The Strangeness That Is Wales

The Strangeness That Is Wales

Jack's Strange Tales Book 3

Jack Strange

'This is Wales. Everybody has a song or a story'
Aelwen Prichard

Wales: the cradle of the British Race
Traditional saying

Wales: the country of origins
Traditional saying

Acknowledgements

I would like to thank the staff at the National Library of Wales, sundry people who directed me to out-of-the-way places in various parts of Wales, a collie dog who kept me entertained at the Devil's Bridge and Mrs Aelwen Prichard, who appeared out of the blue, entertained me with music, anecdotes, knowledge and story and vanished without giving me her address. I would also like to thank my wife, the crazy woman who accompanied me on my aimless wanderings and did not complain (much) when we got sodden wet or extremely muddy as we slithered around strange lakes, plodded along surging rivers and poked through castles and other antiquities.

Contents

Introduction

My name is Jack Strange. A few years ago I wrote *Strange Tales of the Sea* which some people seemed to like and asked why I did not write others. So I wrote *Strange Tales of Scotland,* and *It's a Strange Place, England.* A. J. Griffith-Jones, an author of excellent books suggested that I continue the series with a book on Wales. That task was no hardship as Wales is a country I know and love, so, herein lies some of the strangeness of Wales.

It is possible, if unlikely that somewhere in the world there is some-body who has never heard of Wales. For the benefit of that solitary lost soul, and anybody else who may wish to know slightly more, I will begin this small book with a brief and very personal introduction to Wales, as seen by Jack Strange. Those who already have knowledge of Wales can skip the following few paragraphs.

Wales is a very strange country. It tears at the heartstrings in a way that no other place can save perhaps the Holy Land. Why that should be, I do not understand; it could be the combination of legend, scenery and history interwoven with a certain undefinable atmosphere that permeates the air and the rain and the soul.

Wales calls one back with its unique language, its lovely green land-scapes, its ancient, challenging history and the music of the wind through its valleys and hills. There always seems to be music in Wales. It is in the speech of the people, the tongue-twisting names of the towns and villages, the rousing choruses at the rugby matches and even the surging surf of the stern west coast.

Of all the nations of the political and monarchical union that make up the United Kingdom of Great Britain and Northern Ireland, Wales is the most British, yet still stubbornly uniquely, different. It is the most British because it is the home of the people known as Britons, the descendants of the indigenous inhabitants of these islands. Driven westward by invading Germanic tribes of Angles and Saxons, raided by fierce Irish and pagan Norsemen, the Britons resisted strongly. Welsh history is rich with stories of heroes and warriors who fought against immense, overwhelming odds and who often won.

The Cambrian Mountains form the geographical backbone of Wales; a rugged chain that stretches north and south, creating a dramatic landscape for tales of fairies and monsters, witches and ghosts. South Wales has haunted Tintern, the bustling cities of Swansea and Cardiff, passionate sport and ghost-riddled mines. There is a breathtaking coast in Pembrokeshire, with memories of mermaids and the last invasion of Britain. To the north and facing west is the gentler Cardigan Bay, complete with a vanished land and then, when the visitor thinks he or she has seen the best, they come face to face with Caernarvon and the Druidical island of Anglesey, set against the unbelievably beautiful Snowdonia. Follow the coast eastward to England, and you have encompassed Wales, yet visiting and touring are a long way from understanding. To get to know a place, it is necessary to speak to the people and listen to what they say. One must delve into the past, not only to read the official histories that present carefully considered facts, but to enter the minds of the native inhabitants and discover what they thought and what they believed, the traditions and folklore, the fears and legends that hint of the hidden soul of the land. Until these beliefs of the indigenous population are unveiled, the visitor, whether long or short term, will always be a stranger.

It is hard not to find legends, folklore and myths in Wales. Sometimes they sound like pure fantasy, at other times they are probably based on some event in the far distant past that has passed into folk-memory, altered and twisted by a hundred generations of telling. Sometimes the story is so old there are no words left, only stark rocks, staring at the ragged sky. Such is the case with Mynydd Prescelly, the site of the quarry for Stonehenge, and that in itself is strange. How did people from the flat plains of what is now England even learn of this place, what skills and labour were used to carve out these immense blocks of stone and how much effort was used to transport them so far?

Wales can hide its talents and shield its daughters and sons better than any other nation I know. She portrays herself as a nation of poets and coal miners, where the daffodil and the leek are important and the dragon is her symbol. All that may be true, yet Wales is so much more than that. She is a land of supreme beauty that has produced perhaps more famous people than any other of similar size. Yet often the world does not realise the Welsh heritage of her sons and daughters. Lawrence of Arabia, Henry Morgan the buccaneer, Tommy Cooper the comedian, Roald Dahl the author, King Henry V of England, Robert Recorde the 16th-century mathematician, Geoffrey of Monmouth who wrote of King Arthur, and Aneurin Bevin who invented the NHS. These were some of the famous and not so famous who called Wales their home. Other well-thought-of people have Welsh blood. Did you know that Daniel Boone comes from Welsh stock? His mother, Sarah Morgan, was a Welsh Quaker.

Was a Welshman first to discover America, centuries before Columbus? It is possible, given the nautical history of the Welsh. Was King Arthur Welsh? Wales abounds with Arthurian lore, while Arthur is said to have fought monsters and giants in the north of the county as if fighting invading Saxons was not enough. Is there pirate treasure buried in an island off the Welsh coast? Who was the phantom knight at Tintern? Where is the Lourdes of Wales? There are so many questions in this most strange of countries.

As with every European nation, the boundaries of Wales have altered over time. At one time the whole of what is now Wales and England, plus southern Scotland, spoke the language now called Welsh, although the idea of a single nation state was not then considered. To simplify a complex situation that takes in religion and English national insecurity, in 1536 King Henry VIII's so-called Act of Union fixed the border between a united Wales and England. Tracts of what had once been Welsh land was included in English counties, hence the plethora of Welsh language names in south-west Herefordshire. Village names such as Llancillo, Llandinabo and Llanrothal, all now in England, speak of Welsh heritage. You can take a Welshman out of Wales, but never the Welsh from the landscape. And that begs the question, why do outsiders use the term Wales and Welshmen?

The correct name for Wales is *Cymru*, which is the name the Welsh, the *Cymry*, use for their country. The name *Welsh* is from the Germanic, Anglo-Saxon word *wealh*, which means foreigner. In other words, when the Germanic tribes invaded in the 5th and 6th centuries, they designated anybody not German as a foreigner, thus calling the *Cymry* foreigners in their own country. You can hardly get stranger than that.

Wales is a land of castles, often built by invaders to try and control a people not at all easy to subdue. The invaders, wave after wave of them, from Romans to Saxons to Normans and Plantagenet princes, must indeed have been apprehensive of the power of the Welsh to cower inside such formidable fortifications. Mind you, with warriors such as Owen Glendower and Llewellyn the Great defending Wales, the invaders were very wise to hide behind walls of solid stone.

The Welsh language is not the easiest to read. It is old, it is Celtic, and it has survived centuries of persecution. I will add a short note to help pronunciation. There are only twenty letters in Welsh as opposed to twenty-six in English, with the consonants j, k, q, v, x and z unknown. As a consolation, the letter 'f' is pronounced as 'v' and double f 'ff' pronounced as 'f'. The double 'd' – 'dd' is the same as 'th' and 'll' is similar to 'hl' – you have to hear the sound to be able to say it accurately! Place names are often topographical, with llyn being a lake and bryn a hill.

Here are a few common words that occur in Welsh geography:

Aber – estuary
Afon – river
Bach – small
Bont – bridge
Bwlch – pass
Caer – fort
Capel – chapel
Cwm – valley
Fawr – large
Gwyn – white
Llan – church
Llyn - Lake
Maen – rock, boulder
Mynydd – mountain
Tre – town.

I have tried my best to get the spelling of the Welsh names correct, but it is inevitable that I will have some wrong. For that, I can only apologise and hope for forgiveness.

With cottages with walls of slate to protect them from the weather, beer called Brains, a mining history that stretches from around 2000 BC and includes a plethora of ghosts as well as small helpful knocking creatures, haunted castles and lake monsters; unusual customs and historic symbols, Wales is indeed a country like no other, it is a strange country. It is Wales. *Cymru am byth*! Wales forever!

Chapter One
The Symbols of Wales

DRAGONS, DAFFODILS and LEEKS

Every nation has its national symbols. The United States of America has the bald eagle and the bison, Canada the maple leaf and the beaver, Russia the bear. Wales, being old and Welsh, has three, the dragon, the daffodil and the leek. I could count the Prince of Wales' three feathers, but that is more a royal symbol rather than a national one. Others may disagree, and they could well be right.

Of all the Welsh symbols, the dragon is arguably the best known. Indeed, Wales is the home of the dragon or the *draig* in Welsh. True, many other nations have dragons in various ceremonies and stories, and Saint George is said to have slain a stray dragon in the Middle East, but Wales is so proud of her dragon that she portrays it on her flag.

Not surprisingly, there are many dragon legends in Wales. For instance, there is the story of Vortigern, a semi-mythical Celtic king of around the late fourth and early fifth centuries AD. According to one legend, Vortigern was trying to escape the vicious Saxon invasion and decided to build a castle at the pretty little knoll of Dinas Emrys in what is now Gwynedd in north-west Wales. However, Vortigern's early building works failed, and he was advised that supernatural forces were preventing him from succeeding. The cure for such interference, some wise man said, was to sacrifice a young man. Vortigern searched for a suitable sacrifice and found a lad named Merlin, who told the king that he was a bit silly trying to build a castle on an underground lake that held two sleeping dragons.

In those far-off days, it seemed to be routine to come across the odd dragon in Wales, so Vortigern's labourers dug into the ground until they found the offending creatures. One dragon was red and the other white and as soon as the humans arrived, they began to fight one another. The red dragon was symbolic of the British, or Welsh, while the white dragon was the Saxon or English invaders. Eventually, the red dragon was victorious, and his – or her – victory was taken to prophesy the coming reign of King Arthur. One must remember that King Arthur's father was none other than Uther Pendragon and legend says that Arthur fought under a dragon banner. In this confusing mishmash of legend, myth and fabrication, there may even be a grain or two of truth. Some people say that ever since Vortigern's time, the red dragon has been the symbol of Wales.

Naturally, there is not just a single legend to explain the name of Vortigern's castle. One version of the story claims that Dinas Emrys honours the mystical Myrddin Emrys, often known as Merlin. Other people say that Dinas Emrys means Emrys's Fort, which was another name of Ambrosius Aurelianus, who took after the fort after Vortigern. Legends and myths are never straightforward and often weave in and out of truth, fantasy and possibilities in a Celtic knot that seems determined to confuse the reader.

There was undoubtedly a fort at Dinas Emrys, with Llewelyn the Last (c 1223 – 1282) the final native Prince of Wales, given credit for building it, rather than Vortigern. However, the present ruins are on an older site that dates back perhaps two thousand years, and when archaeologists examined the fort in the 1950s, they found a pool or lake, although the dragons were long gone. What came first, the pool or the legend? Or did some long-forgotten denizen of the fort keep some exotic beast in the pool at some time?

Naturally, there is also a legend telling how the dragons came to be in the pool in the first place. *The Mabinogion*, that fantastic book that contains so much Welsh folklore, is the source. *The Mabinogion* states that when Lludd was king, at a time so distant it was even before the iron legions of Rome arrived, every May Eve the countryside shuddered under a terrible scream. The sound was so fearful that it petrified everybody who heard it, caused miscarriages and killed animals on the spot. Llefelys, the King of Gaul told Lludd that it was the sound that dragons made when they fought. Llefelys claimed that the British dragon was screaming because an invader dragon was defeating it.

To further confuse matters, at that time dragons periodically changed into pigs, so Lludd waited until they altered and trapped both pig-dragons in a cauldron full of mead. An alternative version of the story states that the dragons simply drank the mead and fell asleep, with no mention of pig-changing. Either way, once he had caught both beasts, Lludd buried them at Dinas Emrys. The place where they were held is still pointed out, a stone circle that would predate even the original fort.

One legend leads to another, and then another. We will find a great deal of treasure in our traipsing through Wales, and one hoard belonged to Merlin or Myrddin. He hid his treasure in a cave near to Dinas Emrys and prophesied that when a particular fair-haired and blue-eyed individual approached, he or she will hear a bell, which will lead them into the cave. Naturally, the cave will magically open although it is not clear what happens next. Presumably, the fair-haired individual will squeal with delight at finding so much gold; the mediaeval equivalent of winning the lottery. Also near to Dinas Emrys is Cell y Dewiniaid, a name which apparently means the grove of magicians. Local lore claims that the magicians who gathered here were Vortigern's priests, and they were buried in the neighbouring field. Possibly- and this is tentative guesswork - all these magical happenings were linked to the activities of the one-time Druids who were active in this area and pop up all across Wales. Although oak trees and

Druids are securely connected, folk memory has only retained some blurred and hazy recollections of that ancient religion.

But that is to roam a bit from the Welsh dragons. Laying Vortigern's red-and-white dragons aside, the dragon symbol is ancient and may actually predate the legend. When the Romans occupied the southernmost two-thirds of Britain, they recruited men for their army, and these soldiers appear to have fought under a dragon banner. Some think that Magnus Maximus, a Spanish Roman general based in Wales when the Roman Empire was disintegrating, had the red dragon as his symbol. Other people say that when the Romans withdrew, some British kings used the logo on their flag, hence the Arthurian connection. Or so the legends say - as well as the *Historia Brittonum*, written around 828 AD.

On more concrete historical ground, we have Henry Tudor, who became King Henry VII. This particular royal Henry was born in Pembroke Castle in Wales and was one of the protagonists in the Wars of the Roses. In 1485 as he marched to the battle of Bosworth against Richard III, many Welshmen supported Henry and had the red dragon flying at their head. After the battle was won and the crown secured, King Henry had the Welsh dragon flag blessed in London's St Paul's Cathedral. With typical royal ingratitude, when the 1603 Union of the Crowns came about, only the crosses of Scotland and England were used in the first Union Flag. The red dragon of Wales was left out in the cold.

To further complicate things, there is a rival dragon for the Welsh banner. In Welsh, the red dragon is *Y Ddraig Goch*, while the standard of Owain Glyndwr was *Y Ddraig Aur*, the Golden Dragon. Owain Glyndwr (c 1349-c1416) was a Welsh prince who tried to unite Wales and expel the English. After a string of victories, he was eventually defeated. Details of his death are uncertain, but he remains an influential figure in Welsh minds. Owain Glyndwr raised his golden dragon flag during the battle of Tuthill in 1401, and some think that a golden dragon on a white background was the original flag of Uther Pendragon and Arthur, rather than a red dragon. The present Welsh flag has the red dragon of Cadwaladr ap Cadwallon, set on the green and white Tudor field of Henry VII. In case you did not know, Cadwaladr ap Cadwallon was the king of Gwynedd from the 650s until 682, and fought the encroaching Angles with some astounding success.

As I mentioned above, Wales has a host of dragon legends. In my perambulations around the country, both physically and metaphorically, I located some, and list them below, but undoubtedly there are more.

There is a strange story about Castle Gwys, otherwise known as Wiston Castle in Pembrokeshire, which was the home of a dragon with many eyes. The legend said that if anybody succeeded in spotting the dragon before it saw them, that person could claim the castle and lands. Many people tried, only for the multi-eyed beast to see them first. Eventually, one bright lad hid inside a barrel and had people push him into the castle. Presumably, he peeped out of the bung-hole and saw the dragon first to claim the prize.

Dragons appear to have been tricky things and humans needed to be cunning to defeat them. When a dragon settled into St Teilo's church tower in Llandeilo Graban in Powys, the locals were not happy. They knew that they could not kill the creature in a straight fight, so one man decided to fool it. He made an oaken dragon and booby-trapped it with steel spikes, like a giant hedgehog. The church tower dragon saw this rival and flew down to the attack, only to be pierced by the spikes and die.

That dragon may consider itself to be lucky compared to the dragon of Newcastle Emlyn in Carmarthenshire. This proud dragon lived in the local abandoned castle, and with its thick armoured body, lashing tail and poisonous breath, it thought it was invulnerable. However, like Achilles and Superman, everybody and everything has at least one weakness, and the Newcastle Emlyn dragon was no exception. A local warrior heard where the dragon's weak spot was and worked out how to reach it. He obtained a square of red cloth and waved it around, which annoyed the dragon, which flew down to the attack, grabbed the cloth and flew up again. However, as it soared upward, the warrior had a clear view of the dragon's bottom and shot an arrow right up. That was the creature's vulnerable place. The dragon flew away screaming, as one would with an arrow in one's bottom, and fell into the river. All the poison in its body poured out of the wound and massacred the local fish.

We have not done with dragons yet. Here are a few more bits and pieces of Welsh dragon-lore. In the First World War (1914-1918) Welsh soldiers seemed to adopt, or more likely re-affirm the red dragon as their emblem, and it officially became the Welsh national flag in the 1950s. Being Wales, of course, there is yet another alternative national flag in the old Cross of St David, a gold cross on a black background. However, we are still talking dragons.

In the early years of the 20th century and especially in 1910, the Welsh members of the Houses of Parliament campaigned for the Welsh Dragon to be introduced into the royal standard. A small poem of 1901 stated to the king:

'Oh take me to your Royal arms I pray
And let me stand a flag on
Don't start the royal coaches on their way
Until they've got a drag-on.'

On St David's Day, it was standard practice since 1922 to have the Union flag on the Eagle tower and the dragon on the lower Eastern Tower of Caernarvon Castle, which to the Welsh indicated that the dragon was in a subservient position in its own country. On St David's Day in 1931 the Office of Works again refused to allow the Welsh Dragon to fly above the Eagle Tower, so a group of Welsh Nationalists took matters into their own hands. Hauling down the Union Flag, they hoisted the Welsh Dragon, much to the annoyance of Englishmen and staunch unionists. When the dragon was flown the crowd cheered and clapped. Unfortunately, the authorities hauled down the Welsh flag and restored the flag of union. In 1932 a gathering of Welsh students tore down the union flag and tore it to ribbons.

After the commotion in 1932 Mr Ormsby-Gore MP, Lord Harlech declared that in future the two flags should fly at the same height on St David's Day and the king's birthday. In the 1937 coronation celebrations, the people of Wales were graciously allowed to exhibit their red dragon flag rather than the union flag.

Even in Wales, not everybody approves of the Welsh dragon. In August 1949 at St Mary's parish church in Dolgelly in Gwynedd, the union flag was taken down and the Welsh flag raised. The local bell ringers immediately hauled down the dragon and put the union flag back. Apparently, they objected because they had given the church the union flag in the first place. And in 1955, when the union flag flew above the eisteddfod – the Welsh musical and cultural festival - Welshmen hauled it down and hauled up the dragon, with the excuse that the union flag was flying higher than the dragons that flanked it.

The Welsh dragon then is a prickly creature and not one that it is wise to upset. As Tolkien once said: 'never laugh at live dragons' and the Welsh dragon is very much alive and never to be scoffed.

Other dragons, under different names, may also still be alive. There is a prehistoric tumulus at Trelech a'r Betws in Carmarthen which had a dragon, or rather a gwiber, or flying snake, to protect it, although it has not been seen for some years. I could not locate any stories or legends that relate to any attacks by this creature, unlike the Wybrant Gwiber at Betws y Coed which according to legend once ripped the throat from a man who attacked it, then tossed the unfortunate, and very stupid, attacker into a river.

There are many other legends, such as the dragon of Llyn Cynwych at Dolgellau in Gwynedd, which did not use fire but only the power of its stare to kill. One local farmer waited until the dragon was asleep and then chopped its head off with an axe. The locals buried it nearby. Then there was the dragon that once pestered the village of Llanrhaeadr ym Mochant in Powys. The locals had failed to kill it by the usual methods of sword and spear and hope. As a last resort, they erected a stone pillar, added a layer of spikes and covered the entire edifice with a red cloth. As the whole world knows, the colour red angers bulls and dragons, so the dragon puffed itself up with anger and attacked the booby-trapped pillar. Lunging down without any caution, the dragon impaled itself on the spikes and died.

Would it not be good to have a dragon story where the dragon wins? All this dragon-slaughtering is a bit one-sided.

Finally, there was yet another dragon on Penmynydd in Gwynedd. The local landlord was so unhappy about having cattle, sheep and no doubt sundry virgins eaten by the winged creature that he hired a man to eradicate the pest. After the dragon killer had failed to destroy the beast with sword and lance, he, like others before him, resorted to low cunning. Rather than using a spiked booby trap, the dragon-killer dug a deep pit and placed a brass mirror on the bottom. Naturally, the dragon fell into the hole, saw its reflection and fought itself. When the dragon was tired out, the dragon killer jumped into the pit and chopped off the exhausted creature's head.

As can be seen, most of the dragon stories are short and lack detail. It is possible that they were once longer but time has eroded the content, or perhaps they were always only sound-bites with no more content. It should perhaps not be thought strange that Wales has such a plethora of dragon tales, but rather it would be odd if the land of the dragon lacked such stories.

As well as dragons, Wales has the humble leek as a symbol of nationality. According to some traditions, the ancient Druids used leeks in their ceremonies, but better recorded is a legend that the wearing of the leek dates back to 633 when Cadwallon, king of Gwynedd defeated Edwin, king of Northumbria. Cadwallon was a dominant force in the 7th century at a time that the Angles and Saxons were still pushing their frontiers into the land of the native British. Invading Anglo-Saxons had swept into Wales before Cadwallon stopped them and inflicted defeats first on the Mercians and then the Northumbrians, with the decisive battle at Hatfield Chase, where Cadwallon's men were said to have worn leeks to distinguish themselves from the enemy.

Bede, the Northumbrian priest and historian, called Cadwallon 'the unspeakable leader of the Britons' and a 'raging tyrant' so the Welsh king must have been effective against the Northumbrians. The insults of an enemy should always be counted as praise.

Another tradition says that it was St David who first asked Welshmen to wear leeks for identification as far back as 540 AD. That legend is as good an excuse as any to introduce St David, the patron saint of Wales. In Welsh, he is *Dewi Sant,* and he was born in Caerfai in Pembrokeshire, with Pope Callixtus canonising him in 1120 when the Welsh resisted the Norman invasions of their country. David is the only British national saint to be born in the country he patronises, with Patrick (Ireland's saint) being born in Scotland, Andrew (Scotland's saint) in Palestine and George (England's saint) supposedly a Roman soldier born in Turkey. Saint David had royal blood, with his father a prince and his mother the daughter of a chieftain. Made an archbishop after a pilgrimage to Palestine, David founded a dozen monasteries that were renowned for their austere simplicity. David's best-known miracle occurred when he was preaching at the Synod of Brefi. The crowd was so large that they could not all see or hear him, so he lifted the ground beneath his feet to ensure enhanced visibility.

With so many Arthurian legends in Wales, it is perhaps not surprising that some believed that St David was Arthur's nephew. Strangely St David's Day is not a public holiday, with Prime Minister Tony Blair rejecting pleas for it to be made into one as lately as 2007.

In 17th century London, more than a century after the 'union' between Wales and England, any attempted Welsh celebrations of St David's Day were greeted by jeering English mobs parading through the streets lynching effigies of Welshmen. I am not sure why there was animosity to the indigenous British people celebrating their homegrown saint. A century later St David's Day was celebrated by eating a 'Taffy', which was a gingerbread Welshman astride a goat. Today it is more common to celebrate St David's Day by wearing a daffodil or a leek, with a tradition in Welsh regiments of the British Army for soldiers to eat a raw leek.

On St David's Day 1808 the 23rd Foot, the Royal Welch Fusiliers, were sailing to Canada. It was traditional for every officer to eat a leek, with a decided order of precedence. The older officers and those who had fought on campaigns were allowed a small leek, aided by salt. Officers who had seen at least a years' service but no action had to eat a larger leek without salt. For officers who were celebrating their first St David's Day in the regiment, the largest possible leek was found, and they had to eat every morsel and according to Ensign Thomas Henry Browne, later General Browne 'day after day passes before the smell and taste is fairly got rid of.' There is no doubt of the lasting connection between Welsh soldiers and leeks for in 1917 a Welsh soldier wrote home from the Middle East to say that the 'leeks are as big as gateposts'. The Turks, who were the opposition at the time, referred to the Welshmen as the Blue Devils.

Putting aside the idea that Saint David introduced leeks, there is a more prosaic suggestion that leeks became important when farmers in South Wales helped each other at ploughing time. This community event was cemented by a bowl of communal soup, with each farmer contributing a hat-full of leeks.

One last leek-related suggestion comes from the Battle of Crecy, often celebrated as a great English victory over the French. It was, in fact, an allied army, with English knights, and Welsh and Irish spearmen and Welsh and English archers, which defeated the French and their allies that bloody 26th August 1346. According to the story, at one stage the Welsh archers were camping in a field of leeks when a certain captain Cadwgan Voel ordered them to put leeks in their helmets to better identify them. Shakespeare put it succinctly in *Henry V* act 4, scene 7: 'the Welshmen did good service in a garden where leeks did grow.'

The connection between Wales and daffodils appears to be more recent. In 1912 the press had a lively debate whether the national emblem of Wales should be the 'stinking vegetable' the leek or the 'beautiful daffodil.' As recently as July 1911 when one of the many royal Edwards was installed as Prince of Wales at Carnarvon Castle, he accepted the daffodil as the emblem of Wales.

There is a strange little legend about the coming of the daffodil to Wales. A few thousand years ago the people of northern Spain were experts in ironwork, using charcoal to smelt the ore. One autumn, one of their ships was caught in a storm and driven close to the coast of Wales. The seamen landed and saw the Welsh digging for coal, which they used as fuel.

Naturally the Spanish were curious, never having seen such a product before. They wondered if these strange black stones would be more effective in smelting iron than their native charcoal. But what could they give in exchange? Just stealing the coal was out of the question as the Welsh were ferocious warriors. When the Spanish saw the Welsh worshipping the sun they had an idea; they could not give the Welsh the sun, but they could provide the next best thing, a flower that resembled the yellow orb in the sky. The sailed home and returned with a cargo of daffodil bulbs, which the Welsh accepted as barter, and in time daffodils became the national symbol of Wales.

There is, naturally, a more rational, if less colourful explanation. The Welsh for daffodil is *Ceninen Pedr*, Peter's Leek, and the two names and plants got confused in translation. Personally, I prefer the stranger stories.

Lastly, I shall mention the language of Wales. Welsh is one of the indigenous languages of the British Isles, along with Gaelic and whatever language the Picts of Scotland spoke. However, it has been under attack ever since the invasions of the Germanic tribes of Saxons, Jutes and Angles in the 5th and 6th centuries.

After the 'union' with England in the 16th century, the English language was introduced as the only language allowed in Welsh courts. People using Welsh were banned from holding public office in any land owned by the King of England. The idea may have been to eventually eradicate the Welsh language and probably Welsh culture and national feeling from the land. Similar projects were carried out in Ireland and Scotland, with mixed results.

In the middle of the 19th century, the English education system was also eased into Wales, with monoglot English-speaking teachers. Any child found speaking Welsh was handed a Welsh Not (or Welsh Knot), a stick or plaque or another form of identification which he or she had to hold and pass on to any other child who dared to speak their own language. At the close of the day, whoever was left holding the Welsh Not would be punished. Again, similar traditions existed for Gaelic speakers in Ireland and the Scottish Highlands, and even in my childhood in Scotland, pupils were actively and painfully discouraged from speaking Scots at school.

There was, of course, resistance from Welsh speakers to this strange notion of punishing Welsh children for speaking Welsh in Wales.

No book of strange Wales would be complete without mention of the longest place name in Britain: Llanfairpwllgwyngllgogerchwyrndrobwllllantysiliogogoch – it means 'the church of Saint Mary by the hollow of white aspen, over the whirlpool and Saint Tysilio's church close to the red cave. It is in Anglesey, the ancient Druidical centre and with that name, I shall close this chapter.

Chapter Two
Wales Answer to Nessie

I would wager money that most people in the western world have heard of Nessie, Scotland's Loch Ness Monster, yet relatively few have heard of the afanc, the Welsh equivalent. That is a pity, as the afanc is every bit as mysterious as Nessie and has a long history. There may even be an entire collection of afancs, in different places and nobody is quite sure how the creature looks. Some think it is like a crocodile, others that it is a demon or a small dwarf, somewhat akin to an Irish leprechaun.

Perhaps the afanc is a crocodile shaped demon-dwarf, then? How strange would that be?

Whatever its form, an afanc is said to have lived in Llyn Barfog, the Bearded Lake near Aberdyfi in Gwynedd. King Arthur, who crops up all over Wales, was reputed to have dragged the creature from the lake and killed it. However, possibly the most famous afanc used to live in the pool that bears its name, Llyn yr Afanc, not far from the village of Bets-y-Coed in the Conwy Valley in North Wales. One version of the story runs like this:

Back in the old days when dragons roamed the earth, all men were brave and strong and handsome, and all women were beautiful and virtuous, the people of the Conwy Valley were most distraught. Whenever they planted their crops, or set their cattle and sheep into the fields near the river, the water level rose and flooded the land, ruining the grain and drowning the livestock. They would not have minded so much if these events had been natural, but they were not. A terrible afanc caused them.

Typically in the old days of warriors, some brave knight would arrive and free the villagers of their burdens, but this afanc was a bit too scary even for the wandering heroes. It was a massive beast that smashed through the banks of the river, hence the floods, and it had thick skin that repelled even the spears and lances of knights. In fact, no human weapon could hurt it.

As it could not be killed, some other method had to be found to get rid of the afanc. The elders and wise folk held a meeting to discuss the problem. All the old stories say that 'wise men' held a meeting, with no mention of women. Ha! Since when were Welshwomen backwards in coming forward? I would wager good money that the women gave their advice as well, and probably influenced events more than the men cared to admit. Whoever had the final say, the meeting decided to lure the afanc away from the pool and deposit it in a lake as far away as possible. They chose Llyn Ffynnon Las, by Mount Snowdon as the afanc's new home.

The locals contacted Wales' finest blacksmith to forge an iron chain to hold the afanc, and they borrowed the powerful oxen of Hu Gardan to drag the afanc away. All that remained was to lure the afanc from its pool so they could capture it. As anybody with any dealings with mythology will be aware, dragons, afancs and other savage beasts like nothing better than a beautiful young woman. The locals looked for such a woman, which was not a hard task in Wales, and one woman, a farmer's daughter, volunteered to be the bait.

It must have taken nerves as strong as the afanc's hide for the farmer's daughter to stand by the pool and sing softly to attract the beast's attention. Eventually, her ploy worked, and the afanc exploded from the depths. Even when the monster glared at her, the woman continued to sing until the afanc had left the water and was on land. Rather than eat the woman, the beast rested its head at her side, lulled by the sweetness of her voice. Only then did the men appear with the chains to secure the sleeping afanc. When the creature awoke to find itself securely bound, it reacted with fury, lashing its tail and sliding back into its pool. One version of the tale says that in its struggle the afanc inadvertently killed the farmer's daughter. Other versions do not mention that detail. I will go with the more cheerful version and keep the brave Welshwoman alive, for such courage deserves a reward.

Now Hu Gardan used his oxen to haul at the chains, bringing the afanc back to land, with the local men adding their muscle power. From the river bank, men and oxen dragged the afanc, inch by struggling inch toward Llyn Ffynnon Las. According to the legend, one of the oxen pulled so hard that its eye popped from its socket and its tears of pain created Pwll Llygad yr Ych, the Pool of the Ox's Eye, which proves the truth of the story. Eventually, the procession reached Llyn Ffynnon Las and released the afanc, which leapt into its new home and remains there still. Another version of the tale (there are always 'other versions' in Wales) claims that a warrior named Peredur, son of Efrawg killed the afanc when the oxen hauled it out of the river.

Unlike the Loch Ness monster, which was reasonably quiet between its meeting with St Columba in the 6th century and the introduction of mass tourism in the 20th, afancs popped their heads up in mythology from time to time. One such creature appears in *The Mabinogion*, and in the 15th century, another appeared in a poem by Lews Glyn. This afanc was in Llangorse Lake in Powys, then known as Llyn Syfaddon. It is evident that there are many afancs throughout Wales. No doubt they all share the usual characteristics of such entities and wait for somebody to enter the water, at which point they attack and eat them.

A story with similar characteristics to the Llyn yr Afanc tale comes from Brynberian in North Pembrokeshire, which says that once in the unrecorded past, there was a monster, an afanc in a nearby lake. The legend says that the monster lived in a lake or in a pool in the river and ate sheep and other animals. The villagers decided that enough was enough and used the approved technique for monster-capturing, which was to use a beautiful young woman as bait. Presumably, all these afancs were male, for a female afanc may have preferred a hand-some young man.

Leaving the no-doubt terrified girl on view along the side of the lake, the menfolk of the village waited. The monster appeared, the girl ran, and the men pounced, using chains and ropes to secure the beast. When it was tied, the men attacked with the javelins that Wales was famed for. They killed the monster, dragged it as far from the lake as they could and buried it, or so one version of the story goes. The burial site is known as Bedd-yr-Afanc, which means Monster's Grave or even, more prosaically, Beaver's Grave. The burial chamber may have given rise to the legend as it is an impressive 35 feet long Neolithic cairn enclosing a gallery grave.

Lastly, I will mention water horses, which were known throughout all the Celtic lands of Britain and Wales is no exception. The River Towy at Carmarthen had a water horse that was noted for its fiery eyes and hot breath. Not far away, on the shores of Carmarthen Bay was a grey water horse. As with all these creatures, the Carmarthen Bay horse traps its prey by looking docile and useful. There is one story about a man who hitched the horse onto his cart, only for the horse to drag him and his vehicle under the sea. The River Honddu at Brecon also has a grey water horse. This charming creature used to entice men onto its back and then take them for a mad gallop into the air or over treacherous ground. The moral of this story is if you see a docile looking horse, or any other sort of large animal in Wales, treat it with great caution. In this strange country, it could be anything.

Chapter Three
Ghosts That Never Were

Like monsters, ghosts are universal. I would hazard a guess that every country in the world has its ghost stories, but only Wales seems to have a plethora of stories about non-ghosts, i.e., ghosts that turned out to be people in disguise. These strange events occurred in the 19th century and occupied the attention of the local people for a few days or a few weeks before fading away from public notice, or the culprit being discovered. However, they were important at the time, and undoubtedly they were strange, so I feel justified in including them in this small book. I will begin this chapter with my own introduction into the non-ghosts of Wales.

I was sitting in Scholars pub in Aberystwyth, nursing my pint of Brains and poring over the pile of photocopied and printed documents that the good people of the National Library of Wales had provided for me when a smiling woman sat at my side. Now, I am not normally the recipient of smiles from stray women. Indeed, I am not usually the recipient of smiles from any woman, including my wife: verbal abuse yes and much, much free advice, but seldom smiles, so I responded with a startled death's head grin that must have scared the life out of the poor barman who happened to be watching.

'What are you doing?' The smiling, forthright lady asked me, pointing to the papers I had scattered all over the table.

I told her that I was researching a small book on strange happenings and beliefs in Wales. The lady's smile broadened, and she said that I would find that an easy job.

'You don't need books for that,' she said, with her eyes as bright as the moon over Cadair Idris. 'This is Wales. Everyone has a song or a story. All you have to do is ask the people.'

I could see that this lady wished to talk, so I put my papers aside and asked if she had any stories that were a bit different and not generally known.

'I do,' she said. 'I know some ghost stories that my *Nain* told us.'

'Your *Nain*?' I asked, looking foolish.

'My grandmother,' the lady explained. 'You should learn some Welsh if you want to understand Wales.'

I agreed with her. I should have learned some Welsh.

The lady introduced herself as Mrs Aelwen Prichard, and she happily agreed to me mentioning her name, which was encouraging. I also did a little research later and found some references to the occurrences she mentioned, although without many of the details.

Perhaps it was the influence of the gothic novels of *Frankenstein, Dracula* and the works of Edgar Alan Poe that encouraged people in 19th century Wales to report a high number of ghosts. It was an age when those who believed themselves responsible and progressive sought to distance themselves from what they saw as primitive superstition and scoffed at the ancient beliefs of their ancestors. However old ideas lingered beneath the industrialisation and the veneer of modernity and any mention of ghosts caused a reaction among many people.

Some of the spirits people witnessed may have been real. Others, including most that Mrs Aelwen Pritchard spoke about, most definitely were not.

In October 1887 the good people of Wrexham were in a tizzy. A ghost had suddenly appeared in the cemetery, terrifying those of a nervous disposition, chasing women and children, causing dogs to bark uproariously and generally causing mayhem. Although there were people of a superstitious nature who preferred to avoid the cemetery entirely, others were faintly amused by the spectacle and every night crowds gathered to see what the ghost would get up to next. In the days before television and radio, ghosts were a source of free entertainment.

There was nothing particularly scary about the spectre of the cemetery; dressed in the traditional white shroud, it would glide between the gravestones with its arms raised, vanishing into nothingness whenever people came too close. However, when complaints came in, and the crowds became bothersome, the Wrexham police thought this ghost business was becoming a bit of a nuisance and sent a couple of bobbies to sort things out. The constables waited in the shadows of the cemetery, smoking their pipes, grumbling at the waste of time and waiting for something to happen.

Eventually, they saw movement between the gravestones. Something white was stirring. While one constable stayed put, the other stubbed out his pipe and walked around the ghost. The ghost saw the prowling policeman and made his way in the opposite direction, still waving his ghostly arms in the air and making hopefully-ghostly noises. As soon as the second constable made his presence known, the ghost gave a shriek and glided away. When the two constables closed in on the terrified spirit, it screamed again, tripped over a gravestone and ended up face down on top of a newly dug grave.

Grabbing the shroud, the police ripped it none-too-gently off the flesh-and-blood man beneath and charged him with public order acts. Matthias Davies was fined sixteen shillings with the option of fourteen days in jail.

Mrs Aelwen Pritchard smiled when she told me that little story. She said that if she remembered her mother's stories well enough, the police paraded Mr Davies through the streets in his white sheet to prove to the citizens that there was nothing to be frightened of.

In the late autumn of 1880 Llanelly, or Llanelli, in Monmouthshire also had its ghost rumours. Again the ghost was draped in its white burial shroud, and again it haunted the local cemetery. Stories abounded that this ghost was a bit of a wanderer, taking time off from its usual haunts to stalk Llanelly Park and even venturing onto the streets outside. As usual with such manifestations, there was a mixture of responses, from people who were too frightened to venture near the cemetery to those who gathered out of curiosity. Most of the population, however, carried on with their lives, ghost or not.

However one night in early November, the ghost went too far and drifted close to the Star public house. That was a bit too much even for tolerant Welshmen. A ghost scaring people was one thing, but a ghost interfering with their drinking time was a bit rich. Rushing out of the pub with his pint in his hand, one brave man saw the ghost, shouted, and gave chase. The spirit turned and fled with its white shroud flapping in the breeze and its boots clicking on the pavement.

The drinking man dumped his glass on a handy window-ledge and chased after the fleeing spectre, still shouting. The ghost ran as fast as its ghostly garb permitted but the man proved the faster. He threw his arms around the white figure and wrestled it to the nearest gas lamp, where he ripped off the shroud. The young woman beneath gave him a faint, slightly nervous smile and another false ghost had been laid.

That much of the story, apart from the details of the pint glass, I could confirm from newspaper reports. Mrs Aelwen Pritchard added a couple of graphic details, saying that the young woman tried to escape by flirting with the man, who replied by dragging her to her parents' house and letting them deal with her.

Llangollen in Denbighshire, not far from the English border was another place with a less-than-spiritual ghost. In May 1869 Church Street in Llangollen was plagued by a spirit. In common with many people in Wales, the spirit was bilingual and spoke in both Welsh and English, although without ever making an appearance. It seemed to have chosen one of the houses to haunt and altered its location from the letterbox to the chimney-flue and back. As seemed to be usual in such situations, word spread through the town, and a sizeable crowd gathered in the street to hear the supposed ghost, but not everybody was convinced it was genuine. The sceptics were correct. After they scoured the street, they found a young girl with an uncanny gift for ventriloquism. That was the whole story, and not even Mrs Pritchard could add details. When I asked a couple of Llangollen locals, they were also unable to add more to the story, or what happened to the talented girl. In fact, nobody had even heard the story.

Although it seemed reasonable to call out the police to hunt for ghosts in Victorian Wales, on at least one occasion the army also marched on a dramatic ghost hunt. In March 1901 the people of Wales, together with the rest of the British populace, avidly read the newspapers for the latest reports of the Great Boer War in South Africa. Names such as Spion Kop, Mafeking and Magersfontein were on everybody's lips as the British people became familiar with South African geography. Various militia and volunteer units were getting ready to support the regular army in their operations in the vast African veld, so training was kept up back at home.

Aberystwyth in Ceredigion, then known as Cardiganshire, was no exception. The Volunteer movement had revived as far back as 1859 to face a perceived threat by France and the manhood of virtually every community in Great Britain enthusiastically flocked to don uniforms. By 1901 the Volunteers, the Territorial Army of its day, were well established as part of the military and social scene, with annual camps, dances and shooting competitions. Yet in the early spring of that year, the people of Aberystwyth had other things on their mind as they heard stories of strange things happening on Penglais Hill, now the site of a major road and a university campus. During the day the hill was perfectly normal but after night people and women, in particular, were advised not to go near Penglais. There were questions, of course, why any respectable woman would want to go gallivanting up a hill in the middle of the night. Those women who dared, and who met the ghost, were often too frantic with fear to relate what happened to them, but their dishevelled appearance told its own story.

At this point, Mrs Pritchard shook her head primly and said that, in her opinion, they had asked for all they got for going to a place they knew was unsafe. Then she smiled and said she would have been first up, just to see what was happening.

One of the more articulate women who returned from the hill spoke of a creature with hard hands that slapped her 'on the rump of her skirt' and would have tried even more intimacy had she not screamed and run away. Men were also liable to be attacked, with one unfortunate youth staggering down the hill with blood pouring from his nose and two loose teeth. If it was a ghost, it was a very solid spectre.

It was bad enough having a war thousands of miles away without having a slapping, punching ghost in their own backyard so the members of the Aberystwyth Drill Class, men who might soon join the local Volunteers, decided to clean up the hill their own way. First, they decided who was the smallest and most feminine-looking of the Class and gave him a task that was most unwelcome: he had to ask his older sister a favour. The young man was not happy but agreed, for the sake of the womenfolk of the town.

At nine in the evening of Friday 15th March, the Drill Class paraded outside the barracks, ready for action. The unlucky smallest youth was the butt of jokes as he wore a deep scowl and his sister's clothes in the midst of all the khaki uniforms. The theory was that the ghost, or whatever it was, preferred to attack women, so if one of the Volunteers looked vaguely feminine, he would attract the ghost's attention. When the spirit came for the unwilling volunteer, the other members of the Drill Class would close in and capture it.

According to Mrs Prichard, the friends of the forced cross-dresser had held him down to shave off his much-prized moustache and had glued a long blonde wig onto his head.

Marching away from the barracks and past the workhouse, the Drill Class halted to dress their ranks. The officers ordered that the men advance in extended order, with the wings striding through the fields on either side of the road. If the ghost appeared, the Drill Class would be in a position to catch it. However, despite the temptation of the glowering youth mincing forward in his sister's grudgingly loaned-out clothes, the hard-handed phantom refused to make an appearance.

In fact after the military manoeuvres that evening, the ghost never appeared at all, so perhaps the embarrassment of the cross-dressing soldier was worthwhile.

Mrs Prichard's had been saving her final story up. She arranged to meet me a second time and was waiting in the same pub, although without anything to drink until I arrived. Once again, I listened to her words of wisdom and took notes to check her facts at a later date. Contemporary newspapers confirmed the gist of her words, so I am ready to accept the remainder is genuine, or as valid as any such story ever is.

As the winter of 1855 brought sleet and rain to Wales, and the pubs and firesides were filled with talk about the ongoing war with Russia, strange happenings occurred near Llansamlet, now a suburb of Swansea. It was a Saturday evening in November and Samuel and Mary Evans were on their way home along the bank of the Tennant Canal when they heard an unusual noise.

Neither Samuel nor Mary was sure what the noise was; they only knew that it was unlike anything they had heard before and then, moments later, a *thing* appeared. In the dark and the rain, neither could describe it accurately, but Mary thought it was like a headless pony; she grabbed Samuel's arm, and both ran as fast as they could. They fled uphill to the church, only to see something equally strange hovering against the churchyard wall.

'Run!' Samuel pushed Mary ahead. He was carrying their weekly shopping and knew he would only slow her down. 'You run, Mary, run!'

'How about you?' Mary hesitated, waiting for her husband.

'I'll be all right. Go on!' Samuel pushed Mary again. 'Wake the neighbours; tell them to come and see this thing!'

'Take care, Sam, please take care!' Mary lifted her long skirt and fled, nearly tripping in her efforts to escape the headless thing that infested the road. Although Mary shouted for help, nobody came; it was long past midnight, and the good people were in bed. Meanwhile, Samuel walked on, nervous, maybe scared but still carrying the groceries. He heard the strange noise again and decided that he had no choice. His nerve finally failed him, he thrust the shopping basket under a hedge and ran, to find Mary at home, still shaking yet glad that they were both safe.

The following day, with his nerves calmed down and a group of his neighbours for support, Samuel returned, to find the basket of groceries gone.

'The ghost must have been hungry,' somebody said.

'Either that or some tramp has found your groceries,' a more cynical woman added.

'What will we do for food, Sam?' Mary asked, but they were in Wales, so the neighbours gathered round to help.

After a few days of nervous peace, the ghost returned. Captain Pringle of the brig *Mary's Promise* was loading coals near Crown Works at Port Tennant when he realised that something was following him. More wary of potential thieves than of ghosts, he glanced over his shoulder to see what he thought was a headless dog. Naturally alarmed, Captain Pringle hurried along the dark road. He felt in his pocket, wishing he had brought some sort of weapon with him as the dog transformed into the vague shape of a human before it suddenly vanished. Thankful for his escape, Captain Pringle hurried away to tell people of his strange encounter.

However, he was not alone. Barely an hour passed before the *thing* was back. This time a Mrs Peterson was walking home, carrying a basket of groceries along the same path the captain had used, when the headless dog leapt out on her. Shrieking in horror, Mrs Peterson dropped her basket and fled. When she arrived home, it took her half an hour to calm down before she gathered her friends and hurried back down the road to reclaim her shopping. It was a wasted trip as both the basket and the contents had gone.

By that time the local people realised that this *thing*, whatever it was, was not going away. Opinion was divided between those who believed it was a genuine supernatural phenomenon and the sceptical who doubted that any ghost would steal baskets of food. While the more nervous of the locals were scared every time they left their homes, the more robust were angry at this intrusion. Eventually, a dozen workmen decided to wait for this supposed ghost and see if it was ethereal or corporeal. Talking loudly to give each other courage, they arranged an ambush on the same road down by the Tennant Canal, waiting until after dark on the first Friday night of December.

The walls of the Crown Works were weeping with rain when, around eleven at night, the shapeless *thing* appeared again. Staying close together for mutual support, the workmen thought the *thing* had risen from the waters of the canal, and watched it drift along the tram road, very close to where Mr and Mrs Evans had first seen it.

When the *thing* stopped, the boldest of the waiting workmen slipped from his hiding place and walked towards it, tapping his walking stick on the road. However, his courage failed as he passed and he did not speak. The *thing* moved, approaching him slowly and silently. The workman took a deep breath and asked who or what it was.

'Who are you?'

The *thing* did not reply. It was shapeless, headless and silent in the dismal gloom of the winter night. If anything, it was like a large Newfoundland Dog.

'Who are you?' The workman asked again. When the *thing* still did not reply, the workman made his mind up. 'Well, if you won't answer me, I must feel you, and you shall in return feel me.' Lifting his stick, he thumped the ghost as hard as he could.

Obviously surprised, the ghost drifted away with some haste, which encouraged the other workmen to burst from cover to chase it. The *thing* fled westwards, towards Swansea, still making no noise as it ran, slowed down and sped up again. By that time the workmen were in hot pursuit, now sure that there was nothing in the least supernatural about their quarry. The *thing* passed Red Jacket Pill Junction, and then, near Half Way House, it vanished as if it had never been.

The pursuers stopped running and looked around, gasping for breath. The sudden disappearance of the ghost made some of them doubtful again. What if it was a genuine ghost? Would it haunt them for years? The men grouped together to discuss what best to do just as a crowd of women arrived to give feminine advice and encouragement.

'I think I can hear something,' Mrs Evans said, and sure enough, a few seconds later the ghost appeared again. This time the men were ready and grabbed it before it could escape. Within seconds they stripped the thing of its disguise and found it was very human indeed, an itinerant tinker who lived in a tent near the road he had pretended to haunt.

Now, the meagre accounts I read gave no description of the man, while Mrs Prichard informed me that the tinker was in his late teens or early twenties, 'a handsome enough guy but terribly dirty.'

'What will we do with him?' The men asked themselves.

Dragging the now very reluctant ghost back to the scene of his hauntings, they pondered whether to hand him over to the police or let him go.

Again Mrs Prichard added details here, saying that the women decided that the lad was too young to be sent to jail and they would be better teaching him not to return. Mrs Evans remarked that the ghost could do with a wash.

Possibly on the advice of their wives, the men dealt their own brand of justice. After tying the tinker to a gate, they lowered him into the bitter-cold waters of the Tennant Canal five times, so he emerged soaking wet, freezing cold and half drowned. Some thought that crude water-boarding was punishment enough, but the women were not satisfied, saying that the tinker had terrified them and they wanted proper justice. As the men watched, the women stripped the ghost, turned him face down over the gate and caned him like an errant school-boy. Mrs Prichard had a twinkle in her eye when she told me that Mrs Evans took great satisfaction in applying the cane and who could blame her? After all, it was her weekly shopping that the tinker stole.

And with that little tale of feminine revenge, we leave the realm of strange pretend ghosts and face the strangeness of 18th century warfare.

Chapter Four
Jemima The Great and the French Invasion

In 1797 Great Britain stood alone against the might of Republican France. Having defeated every continental power and with General Napoleon Bonaparte mopping up what resistance remained in Italy, France ruled on land. Even the Pope hastened to pay tribute to the French Juggernaut. The combined fleets of France, Spain and the Netherlands waited to crush the Royal Navy, and to the outside world, Britain seemed doomed. In the meantime, the Directory who ran France planned a devastating raid on Britain to show the impudent islanders what lay in store for them. The Directory imagined that when French soldiers landed, the ordinary people of Wales and England would rise up to help them drive off the oppressive upper classes.

General Hoche's plan was for a three-pronged attack on Britain. He intended some 15,000 men to land in Ireland to fuel the insurrection currently tormenting that unhappy island, with another force landing in Northern England and a third hitting Wales and the English South West. As so often in British affairs, the weather intervened by helping to turn back the intended invasion of Ireland and Northern England, but the assault on Wales continued.

Emptying the jails of some of the most unpleasant people France had produced, the Directory augmented the invasion force with a quota of galley slaves, seared by the lash and hardened by cruel labour, gathered some regular soldiers, found a motley flotilla of ships and ordered them to land in the Bristol Channel. The invaders' orders were to ravage Bristol and create havoc by blowing up magazines and torching docks, knocking down bridges and factories and anything else that may be of use. With western England terrorised, the invaders were to re-embark on their ships and invade Wales, march the full length of the country and menace Liverpool and Chester on the west coast of England. Rather than a full-blown invasion, the Directory intended a raid to spread terror in the belief that having their homes ravaged would encourage the downtrodden peasantry to rise up as the French had done a decade earlier. Politicians have the strangest ideas about ordinary people.

On the 16th February 1797 the four French ships set off for Wales; two frigates, a corvette and a lugger. On board were 1,400 men. Six hundred were French regulars, and the remainder were of *La Legion Noire*, the Black Legion, named after the dark colours of their uniforms, which were captured British uniforms dyed black or dark brown. Officially they were the *Seconde Légion*, but the name the Black Legion sounded more colourful and romantic. The Directory gave command of the raiding force to Colonel William Tate. With a scattering of Irish officers with no love for the British, the men of the Black Legion were reportedly promised a free pardon for their crimes and encouraged to act as they liked in Britain. Raping, murder and looting were positively encouraged. French armies in the Continent lived off booty, so things looked black indeed for the good people of Wales and the English West Country.

There was one thing the French Directory had not considered: the women of Wales.

Colonel Tate was an Irish-American, reportedly born in Wexford although he seemed to have lived in South Carolina. His age has been given as anything from 44 to 70 but is more likely to be closer to the former than the latter. It was also said that he fought against the British during the American Revolution when pro-British Native Americans had killed his parents. How much of that is true, and how much pure imagination is hard to judge. What is sure that he was of Irish stock and at some time had lived in the United States.

The French invasion force sailed into the Bristol Channel on 17th February 1797, giving the unarmed packet boat to Dublin a wide berth in case she was a man-of-war. Tait struck the first blow for Revolutionary France by launching a landing party to destroy an unfortunate farmhouse near Ilfracombe. The smoke of the burning house drifted over the cold Bristol Channel as a distant warning to London; *the French are coming*. Either the British had seen the foreign sails, or news of the landing travelled fast, for the North Devon Volunteers, part-time soldiers with minimal training, grabbed their Brown Bess muskets and hurried toward the invaders. At first sight of the redcoats, the Black Legion scurried back to their ships and headed straight for Wales. Possibly wind conditions made a further landing near Bristol impossible, or Tait's men did not relish a fight quite yet.

On the night of 22nd February, the French landed at Carregwastad Head near Fishguard, the last ever recorded invasion of British soil. Rowing ashore, the invaders lost some artillery and ammunition when an open boat overturned in the choppy seas; the remainder continued. Rather than form a disciplined army, some of the Black Legion at once scattered to rob the local farms and cottages. If the idea was to win hearts and minds to the cause of Revolution, Tait's men had a strange way of showing it.

Lieutenant St Leger and a company of Grenadiers occupied Trehowel Farm on the Llanwnda Peninsula, with Tate moving in shortly afterwards. Some of the Black Legion furthered the French cause by vandalising Llanwnda Church, which would hardly encourage the devout Welsh. However, the 600 French regulars kept their discipline and remained a formidable force. The others, the Black Legion, either deserted, disobeyed orders, got drunk or combined all three. Naturally, the local Welsh civilians resented these drunken buffoons causing mayhem in their country and retaliated, with casualties on both sides. Meantime, the French women were stirring as their anger mounted. Reaching for their red cloaks and tall black hats, they prepared their own fightback.

The local landowner, John Campbell, Lord Cawdor, no doubt pleased to show his military mettle, drummed up all the official local defenders, the Cardigan Militia, the Castle Martin Yeomanry and the 300 strong Fishguard and Newport Volunteers. Only the Militia were full-time soldiers, and all the units had been raised purely for home defence. At around 500 men, Cawdor's combined force was far fewer in number than the French, but still, the Welsh redcoats advanced to defend their homeland. Captain Longcroft of the Royal Navy also did his bit, gathering together the local press gangs and the men of two revenue cutters; Longford armed Haverfordwest Castle with half a dozen cannon and readied another three to send to Cawdor's men.

In the meantime, Tate advanced very slowly through the Welsh countryside and on the morning of 23rd February stationed his men on the hillocks of Carngelli and Garnwnda. Tate was not devoid of military skill for this station gave him both an excellent defensive position and a splendid view of the green land he hoped to suborn. While some of the locals fled the area, most grabbed what weapons they could and rushed to Fishguard to reinforce the Volunteers. And a woman named Jemima Nicholas felt her anger rise.

Cawdor and his now 600 men marched toward the French, who were waiting in an ambush, veteran professional infantrymen with calloused fingers curled around the triggers of their muskets. As night fell, Cawdor decided it was too dark to advance and halted until morning when he could see more clearly. As the two small armies manoeuvred, the French ships sailed away, leaving Tate and his men alone, with a British force of unknown strength pressing them. Abandoned in a strange land and with the expected local support not forthcoming, the Irish and French officers advised surrender. A party rode to Cawdor's headquarters in the Royal Oak public house and offered a conditional surrender. Cawdor said only an unconditional surrender would do, or he would attack. On the morning of the 24th February, Cawdor advanced onto Goodwick Sands against the French force that still outnumbered him. In the afternoon Tate surrendered.

Or that is the official history.

Now, you may well be thinking, that is all well and good and a brief look at military history, but what place does it have in a book about strange Wales? Well, there is another and stranger version of events after the French landed in Wales. There is the story of 47-year-old Jemima Nicholas, or 'Jemima Fawr', Jemima the Great, a local cobbler woman who grabbed a pitchfork and went looking for the invaders. According to folklore she saw a round dozen of the invaders, captured the lot, drove them at the point of her pitchfork to St Mary's Church and had them safely locked up. Mrs Prichard added some picturesque and possibly apocryphal details, such as Jemima drinking from one of the Frenchmen's bottles as she drove them with sharp pitchfork pricks into tight breeches and singing a Welsh song to summon help.

Does that sound a bit far-fetched? Samuel Fenton, the Vicar of Saint Mary's, did not seem to think so when he commented in 1832:

This woman was called Jemima Fawr or Jemima the Great from her heroine acts, she having marched against the French who landed hereabout in 1797 and being of such personal powers as to be able to overcome most men in a fight. I recollect her well. She followed the trade of a shoemaker and made me, when a little boy, several pairs of shoes.

The image of middle-aged women driving a bunch of looters before her with a pitchfork is one to gladden the heart. However there is also an tale that claims Tate's men saw a group of Welsh women in their traditional red cloaks and tall black hats. Either because the Black Legion was befuddled with drink, or because they were soldiers of the most mediocre quality imaginable, they believed the Welsh women were British reinforcements. According to local lore, which is often more accurate than official documents that praise establishment figures and ignore the 'little people', Jemima Fawr led these women round and round Bigney Hill, appearing and disappearing before the eyes of the invaders. The Black Legion and the French regulars saw these red-coated figures in the distance and - the tough invaders immediately surrendered.

Another piece of strangeness surrounds the document of surrender. According to legend, this piece of paper mentioned 'several thousand' British troops that simply did not exist, but the words do lend credence to the story about the women.

However, this little skirmish did have other strange repercussions. For a start, it occasioned a run on the Bank of England, with customers demanding that the bank hand over gold in return for bank notes. That same month parliament passed the Bank Restriction Act, stopping such transactions. The encounter also enabled the Pembroke Yeomanry, now the 224 (Pembroke Yeomanry) Squadron, Royal Logistic Corps, to sport the battle honour *Fishguard*, making them the only unit of the British Army to boast an honour for a battle in the mainland of the UK. It sits strangely beside the battle honours won by other Welsh regiments that include Minden, Alma, Lucknow, Kohima, Malplaquet, Waterloo, Somme and Arras, but if Fishguard had not been won, who knows what horrors the Black Legion might have unleashed?

The invasion has not been forgotten in Wales, for 200 years after the incident, 78 volunteers created the 100-foot long Last Invasion Tapestry. Jemima Nicholas or Niclas (1755 – 1832) has a Commemoration Stone in St Mary's Church in Fishguard, raised in 1897. The story that she led a column of women round and round Bigney Hill is said to be apocryphal. Personally, I would like to believe that a 47-year-old Welshwoman gathered her friends, ensured they were dressed in red cloaks and tall black hats and marched them, like the Duke of York, up the hill and down again to fool Tait's Black Legion. It would make an excellent if strange story. It would also tie in with the fact of the surrender document.

Jemima am byth! Jemima for ever!

Chapter Five
The Devil's Bridge

Nowadays it is unlikely that you will meet the devil when you visit Wales. You may see a rugby game, a flock of sheep or the busy shopping centres of Cardiff and Swansea, but not the devil. Either he does not get round to Wales anymore as he is so busy hobnobbing with his friends in Westminster, or he is still embarrassed at what happened last time he ventured onto Welsh soil.

It was at the beginning of the 11th century, about a thousand years ago, that the devil arrived in Wales. According to one story, he was wandering about the country, grooming his tail and wishing the rain would stop, when he came across an old woman who stood on the bank of the river Mynach in Ceredigion, crying heavily.

Being in devilishly good humour, His Satanic majesty asked the woman what the matter was. She told him that her cow was across the river and she could not cross to get her back. She pointed to her cow, grazing on the lush opposite bank of the Mynach, with a deep chasm and a series of five waterfalls roaring between them.

Scenting a fresh soul to torment, the devil struck a bargain. 'Tell you what,' he said, or the 11th-century equivalent, 'all you need is a bridge.'

'That is so,' said the old woman, no doubting that this stranger was stating the obvious.

'I can make you one,' the devil said, 'but in return, you must agree to do me a favour.'

The old woman, with one eye on her errant cow and the other on the roaring white torrent at the bottom of the chasm, asked what the favour might be.

'It's very simple,' said the devil, smoothly. 'I'll build you a bridge if you agree that I get the soul of the first living thing to cross it.'

The old woman hardly took time to consider her reply. 'All right,' she said. By now she had an inkling who or what this helpful smooth-tongued stranger might be. After all, how many travellers could build a bridge overnight?

In the morning the old woman returned to the river bank, bringing her old and limping dog with her, a handful of biscuits and a loaf of bread for her breakfast. As the devil had promised, a beautiful bridge crossed the torrential river, built of stone and able to survive even the stormiest of winter storms. On the opposite side of the river, the woman's cow continued to graze in perfect contentment. It is strange that nobody thought to work out how the cow crossed the river in the first place. Possibly the fairies lifted her there.

The devil was waiting, smiling at the prospect of soon having another soul to take to hell with him. 'I kept my side of the bargain,' the devil said. 'I know that you will keep yours.'

'I will,' the old woman said. Taking the loaf of bread from under her arm, she took a bite and then tossed her biscuits across the bridge. Her old dog immediately rushed after its breakfast, becoming the first living thing to cross.

The devil was most annoyed. He did not want the scabby old dog; he wanted a juicy human to baste, and he had failed to capture her. Raging, he left Wales and, according to some accounts, he was so ashamed at having been outwitted by an old woman that he never came back.

And that is how the devil's bridge was built. It still stands, a few miles inland from Aberystwyth, crossing the picturesque gorge in the hills. To see it, particularly after an autumn deluge one can understand why people believed that the devil built it.

Naturally, there have been changes in the last thousand years, and two newer bridges have been built above the original. However, it is the lowest one, the Devil's Bridge, which grabs the attention of the visitors. There is another legend that states it is dangerous to cross the bridge during the hours of darkness, for the devil may try and push you off to get even with the old lady who fooled him. So you can't say that Strange Jack did not warn you. If you do venture there, and you hear the sound of hammering from beneath the bridge, don't worry too much for it is only a harmless ghost. The poor wee thing was living or existing anyway (do ghosts live?) in a nearby house, and a priest exorcised it to a cavern under the bridge.

Unfortunately for the legend, the Welsh name for the bridge is Pontafynach, which merely means: 'bridge over the River Mynach.' Even more boring, the devil was not involved in the building process. Quite the reverse in fact as credit for that goes to the monks of nearby Strata Florida Abbey. These godly men may not have been pleased to hear people praise the devil for work they did.

Although the devil may have learned to avoid Wales, he was not forgotten. There is some excellent climbing at the Devils Kitchen in Snowdonia, and there is always Salem to visit.

Aha, I hear you say. Jack, you strange man, you got that wrong. Salem is in Massachusetts in the United States. The witches must have cast a spell or transported it on their corgi dogs to take it to Wales. Well, there is indeed a Salem in Wales, and it well deserves to be thought of as strange.

There are three Capel Salems in Wales, with *Capel* meaning chapel. The one that concerns us was depicted in a picture painted in 1908 that became one of the best-known images in Great Britain. The artist was an Englishman named Sidney Curnow Vesper, but he had the good sense to marry a Welsh woman, Constance James of Merthyr Tydfil. Vesper's picture of Capel Salem became famous when Lord Leverhulme, owner of Lever Brothers, the late Victorian soap makers, used it as a marketing aid. When a customer bought seven pounds of soap, he or she could claim the free gift of a copy of the Salem picture, which shows the interior of the chapel.

I can nearly hear my readers gasping with astonishment at that, and wondering what the devil that has to do with the matter at hand. Well, let me explain. The painting shows the busy interior of Capel Salem, in Pentre Gwynfryn in Gwynedd with one central figure wearing a shawl. Some art admirers believe that the picture is an example of Welsh religion and national dress. Others have different ideas about the image.

For instance, the central female figure is seen walking down the aisle but the clock painted on the wall indicates that it is nearly ten o'clock; the woman, Sian Owen, is therefore late for service. She is also wearing a far more colourful shawl than the others in the congregation which suggests she is highlighting the sin of vanity. If people look hard enough, they can see a picture of the devil in the shawl. Mind you, they will have to twist their head to one side or lean over a lot and screw up their eyes. I could not see it at all until my ever-loving wife pointed out the salient features, with gentle encouragement to me to buy a new pair of glasses.

If anybody wishes to view this devilishly clever picture, the original is in the Lady Lever Art Gallery at Port Sunlight. It is possible that the devil had to hide in the folds of the shawl because he was still ashamed to be seen near his bridge.

Chapter Six
The Welsh Discovery of America

It is strange that history provides so many claimants for the discovery of the American continent. The Italian known as Christopher Columbus is often given the honour, for his was the first most publicised voyage, yet Norse settlements pre-dating Columbus by centuries have been unearthed in eastern Canada. A Scottish nobleman named Sinclair has often been mentioned as having crossed the pond in the fourteenth century, and Celtic monks from Iona may have ventured that far in their leather curraghs. Millennia earlier, of course, the Native Americans were the real first discoverers, either crossing from Siberia or arriving by sea from the west.

However, there is a persistent legend that Prince Madog ab Owain Gwynedd also made the journey in the 12th century. At that time most European eyes were looking eastward to Outremer, where the Crusaders were battling Islam for control of the Holy Land. Wales had her own problems, with the Anglo-Normans continually pressing on the Marches and a lack of unity within the Welsh princes. With so much happening and so many dangers on all sides, it was no wonder that the thought of crossing the western ocean was not immediately uppermost in anybody's mind. Except perhaps in the mind of Prince Madog, or Madoc.

The story begins with Madoc's father. Owain Gwynedd, king of Gwynedd, was a notable man in his day, who argued long and hard with his powerful neighbour, Henry II, King of England. Owain was also a fertile man who produced nineteen children, with six of the offspring in wedlock and thirteen outside. The best known was Madog, more commonly known as Madoc. This Gwynedd prince was apparently born outside the marital bed in Dolwyddelan Castle, not far from the present-day tourist town of Betws-y-Coed, North Wales. According to legend, Madoc was a bit of a strange prince and rather than the usual royal pursuits of hunting, chasing women and fighting, he preferred to spend time with the ordinary people of the land. In particular, he befriended the fishermen. He spent many hours at sea, learning the mysteries of ocean currents, the intricacies of knots, sheets and splices and the lore of the ocean.

In 1170 King Owain died, and his children began to dispute the succession. The chief rivals were Dafydd and Hywel, the eldest two of Owain's many sons. Such divisions were typical in the Middle Ages and frequently led to a pointless and bloody civil war. Two of the brothers, Madoc and Rhirid stepped back from this ugly war of attrition and decided to take ship overseas and leave the squabbling to their siblings. The idea might have been Madoc's as he had the nautical knowledge.

The brothers sailed left from the mouth of the River Ganol and headed west in two vessels named *Gorm Gwynant* (or possibly *Gwennan Gorm*) and *Pedr Sant*.

In the 12th century, what would the ships be like? If it were based on the Norse longboat, it would be clinker built, single-masted, seaworthy and fast. We know nothing at all about the legendary voyage except that it was successful. According to legend, Madoc crossed the Atlantic and landed in what is now Alabama in North America. Evidently liking what he found, he returned for reinforcements and sailed back across the pond. He was never seen again. So much for the sailing legend; could it be true? Or is it entirely false?

Well, according to a continuation of the legend, the Welshmen fostered friendly relations with a Native American tribe, intermarried and settled there, so that stories of a tribe of Welsh-speaking Native Americans circulated for decades. How likely is that?

Welshmen were excellent seamen, of that there is no doubt. If they used Norse style vessels, they would undoubtedly have the ability to cross the Atlantic. Could they have friendly relations with the indigenous population? Why not? A few hundred years later many Scots, mainly Highland Scots, integrated with the Native Americans; their culture and traditions were not dissimilar. In the 12th century, the Welsh would be family and warrior orientated, as were the American tribes, so both sides would understand the culture of the other.

The legend of Madoc persisted for centuries, no doubt helped when the propagandists of Elizabethan England utilised it to undermine Spain's claim to have discovered North America before any other European nation. If the Welsh, coming from a country later ruled by Queen Elizabeth, had established a colony in the Americas centuries before Columbus voyage, then the Spanish claim was spurious at best.

Was there any proof for the Welsh claim? Perhaps. According to one version of the legend, Madoc sailed from Afon Ganol in Penrhyn Bay. As mediaeval ships were of shallow draft, they could quickly have been launched from a beach or even a river. However, a ship large enough to carry colonists and their supplies and food across thousands of miles of Atlantic would have to be larger than average, so may have required some sort of harbour in which to be loaded. In the 1950s the remains of a harbour from the Middle Ages were discovered near Rhos on Sea. Was that where Madoc departed Wales?

When the later European colonisers pushed further into the American mainland, they encountered various indigenous tribes whose language could have evolved from mediaeval Welsh. One such was the Mandan nation – Mandan, Madoc? Perhaps. As the Mandans also used boats that were similar to the Welsh hide-covered coracles, there were other similarities. In the legend, Madoc landed at Mobile Bay in Alabama and took his ships up the Alabama River. If the ships were of the Norse pattern, robust and of shallow draught, such inland penetration was totally feasible. Norse ships often sailed up rivers. To deepen the legend, Alabama has some stone buildings that the 18th century Cherokees apparently claim were built by white people called Welsh.

Sadly, these stories are only stories, and there appears no genuine connection between Prince Madoc and the Mandan or any other Native American people. However, for a time the people of Mobile Bay in Alabama believed the legend and erected a plaque that read:

In memory of Prince Madoc, a Welsh explorer who landed on the shores of Mobile Bay in 1170 and left behind, with the Indians, the Welsh language.

Apparently, that plaque is also now gone. Why are people so disinclined to believe that a Welsh prince should sail the Atlantic? After all, six centuries previously Welshmen and women sailed to found a colony in Brittany and in the 19th century Welshwomen and men sailed to Patagonia. Personally, I can see the logic in men and women escaping from fratricidal war by navigating to a new land. Strange Jack would believe in Madoc.

Chapter Seven
Is This the Strangest Village in the World

It was my wife that wanted to visit Portmeirion, so I blame everything on her. I blame her for the long drive from Northern Scotland to Northern Wales, the queues at the car park, my wet feet at the curiously soft sand at the beach and the wasp sting in a strangely inaccessible portion of my anatomy. I should forgive her, I suppose, for in return I was introduced to one of the most delightful and unique villages that I have ever seen and a place to which I have returned on more than one occasion since.

For people of my generation, this small village in north-western Wales is synonymous with one thing: the seventeen-episode long television series *The Prisoner*. That series was iconic, disturbing and undoubtedly strange. It was a reflection of everything that society was and could be, with the example of one man who refused to lose his individuality to the demands of a faceless state.

The background to this story was the village of Portmeirion. It is difficult to describe Portmeirion; even if one views pictures and videos of the village, the uniqueness is only hinted at. Situated between hills and the sea, Portmeirion has a beach of soft and strangely sinking sand, a concrete boat moored by a tidal river and architecture that would suit Tuscany rather than the west coast of Wales. It is a village like nowhere else in Great Britain and possibly like nowhere else in the world. It is the only village that I have ever had to pay to enter, and a place that owes its existence to the dreams of one man.

Painted in a variety of pastel colours, the architecture of Portmeirion has no single style, pattern or system, yet somehow the array of strange buildings creates a harmony that pleases the eyes. There are domes and a rotunda, an Italianate tower and a bandstand, areas of lawn and flowers and throngs of visitors. It is a seductive place with its own atmosphere which is nothing like the consistently sinister Village in Patrick McGoohan's television series. Having said that, there is no doubting the eccentricity of Portmeirion; in its own way it is the strangest place in Wales, yet in attractiveness, it could be said to vie with Snowdon.

Set in such an ancient country, Portmeirion is surprisingly modern. Clough Williams-Ellis began to build it in 1925 and finally finished as late as 1976. Williams-Ellis built the village piece by piece, in many cases using recycled material from various different places. It is a village that bombards the senses with styles and colours, atmosphere and taste. It is a hodgepodge of delight, a tribute to the skill of Williams-Ellis and a place that has to be savoured. There is too much to accept on a single visit.

For example, the Town Hall itself would be worthy of attention in any urban centre in the country. The plaster interior is a Jacobean masterpiece showing the twelve labours of Hercules. When the plasterwork was on auction in 1933, nobody wanted it so it could well have been destroyed. Williams- Ellis parted with £13 and shifted the whole shabang to Portmeirion where it fits in perfectly. It is priceless. The entire village is like that, a place of nooks and crannies, arched doorways and splendid vistas, stately trees and curious flights of steps leading to more discoveries. A visit here is a trip inside the architectural fantasies of an eccentric genius. My wife and I were lucky that our first visit coincided with a day of brilliant sunshine that filled the courtyards and open spaces with families, laughing children and smiles. I have never visited Portmeirion on a drab day; perhaps the magic of the village even extends to the weather? Now that would be strange for a place on the fringes of the Irish Sea.

The legacy of *The Prisoner* lives on; with a gift shop and a life-size black-and-white representation of Patrick McGoohan, with open cars such as were used in the television series and a whole host of visitors. Portmeirion is a place for families to visit and adults to wonder, of palm trees and flower-beds, of hidden little temples and the high skies of Wales smiling down. There is a small train to take visitors on a trip around the village, and dappled ponds to reflect the clouds above,

Mystical, magical, wonderful, and unforgettable: it could only be Wales.

Yet even before Clough Williams-Ellis brought his influence to bear, Portmeirion was known for its strangeness. A lady named Mrs Adelaide Emma Jane Haigh lived in what is now the Hotel Portmeirion and believed that everything living deserved life, even weeds. The gardeners among us can cringe at the thought of the grounds of Portmeirion with rampant weeds and uncontrolled foliage. Mrs Haigh was also a devout Christian lady. Every day she read her Bible to the fifteen dogs that lived in the Mirror Room in her home. Dogs being creatures who crave attention, I can imagine them crowding round, tails slowly wagging as they placed their noses on the ground to listen.

Although Mrs Haigh is long gone, the cemetery she kept for her dogs can still be seen. She was not the only eccentric who lived in this area for Sir William Fothergill-Cook was her opposite in some ways. Rather than allow plants to live free, he believed in tightly controlling access to his foliage and demolished the 12th century Deudraeth Castle purely to prevent people trampling over his precious plants. Historians, please cringe now. Gerald of Wales mentioned this native-built castle; the present building is strange in its own way but is a mere child by comparison.

Finally, I will mention three more personalities who at one time called Portmeirion home. In no particular order, there was Thomas Edwards; an ex-soldier who was hanged in 1892 for murdering a woman he thought was a prostitute. Apparently, he had intended going to Newport to murder more prostitutes but could not afford the fare so handed himself to the police instead. Then there was the flamboyant Noel Coward who wrote *Blithe Spirit* while he was here and lastly a gentleman with the nearly Dickensian name of Uriah Lovell. He was an old-fashioned gypsy of the wandering variety, and when he died, his body was placed in his caravan, and the whole lot burned. And with that near the Viking-like funeral, I shall bid Portmeirion a very fond au revoir. It is not goodbye forever for I surely will return.

Chapter Eight
The Druids of Anglesey

Ynys Mon, otherwise known as Anglesey is Wales' largest island at 276 square miles. It is a place worth a few days of anybody's time for the strangeness that is woven into the atmosphere and fabric of the island. Some may not see it, but for those with the ability, or the power, to sense what lies beneath the surface, Anglesey is a place unique and sometimes even disturbing. First, a short paragraph about the name.

Anglesey sits on the North West coast of the country, and with Thomas Telford's Menai Suspension Bridge and the Britannia Bridge connecting her to the mainland, may not be considered a true island any longer. Many people will hotly and quite justifiably dispute that claim. The origin of the name is also disputed, with some saying that *Ynys Mon* could mean the Island of Mon, with Mon being a Welsh princess. Sometimes the island is known as *Môn, Mam Cymru*, Mona, the Mother of Wales, or could take her name from an ancient goddess named Modron, the Mother of Wales. You pays your money and takes your choice.

Some hopeful people think that Anglesey may have been the Arthurian Avalon, from the Welsh *Afallach*, - bountiful in apples. Apparently, in the early Celtic period, Anglesey was famed for its apple production. The 12th-century cleric and author Geoffrey of Monmouth certainly named Anglesey *Insule Ponorum*, Island of Apples.

The first time I visited Anglesey it was raining, a thin drizzle that smeared across the Menai Strait and drained all colour from the island. Even so, there was no doubting the drama of the place. This island has an atmosphere that transcends rationality. For those with the ability to empathise with a sense of place, Anglesey is hard to beat. The feeling of the old long-gone people who were here is tangible; it is in the fields and the ancient stones, it creates the island as much as the landscape for this was the home of the Druids.

The human population of the island stretches back for many centuries to pre-history, with a variety of menhirs (upright standing stones) and cromlechs (megalithic altar-tombs). It has been said that Anglesey has more ancient sacred monuments per square mile than anywhere else in Britain. They are everywhere. For example, the burial chamber at Bryn Celli Ddu is fascinating with its passage into the mound while the standing stones at Din Dryfol are an invitation to wonder.

So where are the Druids? They were not involved with raising these ancient stones, yet it was as a Druidical religious centre that Anglesey entered recorded history. When the Romans invaded Britain, they rolled up the tribes in what was now southern England but found resistance stiffer as they marched north and west. In what is now Wales the tribes of the Ordovices, Silures and Demaete were tough to face. The Roman juggernaut, victorious from the banks of the Euphrates to Nubia and from the Atlas Mountains to the Aral Sea, stalled at the Welsh frontier.

The Romans found that the Druids, the religious order of the Celts, organised the resistance against them. Rome was fascinated by the Druids, and Roman writers mention the Druidical oral knowledge and their influence as priests, healers, divines and seers. The chief centre of the Druids was on Anglesey, so around AD 61, General Gaius Suetonius Paulinus marched an army to remove this religious menace.

So who or what were these Druids that required an entire army of the most successful military power in the world to subdue? Well, the truth is that nobody is sure. There are various rumours and wild speculations, but as the Druids left nothing in writing, historians have to rely on the words of the Druids' enemies, which is never a reliable source. We know the Druids were a dominant religious force that seemed to surmount any tribal loyalty and as such were the glue that bound the Celtic peoples together. Perhaps because of the presence of the Druids, Anglesey became a haven for refugees escaping Roman rule and possibly also a rallying place for warriors desperate for the opportunity to strike back. It is significant that the Romans only persecuted two religions, presumably those that they viewed as a threat. One was Christianity, and the other was Druidism, which speaks volumes for the power and influence of the Druids.

Tacitus, a Roman writer, gives the only recorded account of what happened when Suetonius Paulinus:

Prepared accordingly to attack the island of Mona, which had a considerable population of its own, while serving as a haven for refugees; and, in view of the shallow and variable channel, constructed a flotilla of boats with flat bottoms. By this method the infantry crossed; the cavalry, who followed, did so by fording or, in deeper water, by swimming at the side of their horses.

So much for the Romans. On the Druid's side:

On the shore of Anglesey stood the adverse array, a serried mass of arms and men, with women flitting between the ranks. In the style of Furies, in robes of deathly black and with dishevelled hair, they brandished their torches; while a circle of Druids, lifting their hands to heaven and showering imprecations, struck the troops with such an awe at the extraordinary spectacle that, as though their limbs were paralysed, they exposed their bodies to wounds without an attempt at movement. Then, reassured by their general, and inciting each other never to flinch before a band of females and fanatics, they charged behind the standards, cut down all who met them and enveloped the enemy in his own flames.

It sounded more like a massacre than a battle as the veteran, professional Roman soldiers slaughtered the priests, warriors and women of the Druids. Once the Romans had disposed of the Druids, they set about cutting down the sacred groves. According to Tacitus – hardly an unbiased writer - the Druids sacrificed people within the groves and used human entrails to foretell the future. Is this true? Imperialist armies often use propaganda to justify their actions, showing their enemy in the worst possible light. Without a corresponding account from the British point of view, we cannot tell fact from downright lies. What we do know is a mixture of supposition and guesswork mingled with Roman writings and archaeological finds (with apologies to any modern day Druid who may somehow have genuine knowledge of the subject.)

I have read stories of Druids hiding in trees to cut off the heads from marching Roman soldiers. I have never seen these accounts in trustworthy primary sources. Perhaps I have looked in the wrong places.

The Druids seem to have been nature worshippers, with trees central to their beliefs. Yew and oak trees were especially important, and some people believe that the word Druid, *Derwyddon* in Welsh means 'oak knowledge'. Others believe it means 'forest sage' or 'strong seer'. While human sacrifices may be only a Roman invention, there is no doubt that other objects were religiously sacrificed in Anglesey.

When Llyn Cerrig Bach (Lake of the Small Stones) was drained in the 1940s to make an RAF runway, it was found to contain many ancient artefacts from swords and spears to cauldrons, a trumpet and currency bars. The ominous inclusion of slave chains is as a reminder that the Celts were not an innocent pastoral people who indulged only in nature worship, but a warlike society with their own dark side. However, compared to the Roman culture of industrial slavery and ritual sacrifice in their euphemistically styled 'games' the Celts were relatively innocent. The Roman Colosseum was only one of a large number of amphitheatres where animals and humans were sacrificed in unpleasant ways to provide entertainment for a people who were a long way from our notion of civilisation. Perhaps the Romans lived in cities, but cities based on slavery. The Druids would know the reality of Rome, where defeat meant subservience to a brutal new society; it is no wonder they resisted so fiercely.

We do not know how effective the Roman attack on Anglesey was in ending the power of the Druids. We do know that Druidism as a religion survived, for when Saint Columba travelled through the lands of the Picts he met Druids. There is no doubt that Druidism persisted then, in some form, even after Rome's ravaging of Anglesey. The Druids peep out of the pages of this book now and then and many of us, knowingly or unknowingly may possess some Druidic lore.

The Druids were not only in Anglesey, of course. Not far from Penmaenmawr on the North Wales coast, there is a circle of low stones sometimes called the Druid's Circle. In the centre of the circle was a cist, which contained the body of a child. The circle also has the Deity Stone, which thumps anybody who dares to use bad language beside it. I did not try that, just in case. Nearly directly opposite is the Stone of Sacrifice, which has a curious small depression on the surface. The story goes that if a mother lay her very young baby within the depression, he or she would have a life of good fortune. Apparently, on wild nights yells and cries come from the Stone of Sacrifice and according to legend, there was once a witches gathering at these stones where some of the witches touched the stone. Two apparently died, and another lost her mind. Were the Druids involved? Or is this just a scare story? Probably the latter.

I will take a slight leap now to a man who reinvented Druidism for the modern world. His name was William Price, and he was a Welshman, he was born in Wales, lived in Wales, lived *for* Wales and left an indelible mark that continues today. Born in Rudry near Caerphilly in March 1800, William Price is remembered for his part in pushing neo-Druidism, although he was also a medical doctor, a Chartist, a Welsh nationalist and a proponent of cremation.

Although Welsh, Price's father was a Church of England priest, who had married a Welsh maidservant. Such a class-crossing union was frowned on in respectable circles and may have influenced young

William Price in his life choices. It is also possible that eccentricity was in his genes, for Price's father had his moments of strangeness, including bathing in local ponds, with or without clothes and carrying a pocketful of snakes.

After training as a doctor in London, William Price returned to Wales in the 1820s. After a few years at Glyntaff near Pontypridd, Price moved to a farm at nearby Upper Boat and then took on a position as chief surgeon at the Brown Lenox chain works, also near Pontypridd. In 1823 he moved to Treforest. All these villages were in industrialised areas, where working men clustered together in poor conditions. In Treforest, Price judged the Eisteddfod's competition for a bard and joined in the People's Charter movement, which aimed at significant suffrage improvements. Price also gave Welsh lessons to counter the spread of the English language in Wales and joined a Neo-Druidical group named the Society of the Rocking Stone. The Society of the Rocking Stone held their meetings Y Maen Chwyf, a large stone within a circle that had a history of Neo-Druidism rather than a deep understanding of the original Druids.

An 18th century Welshman, Iolo Morgannwg, had hoped to revive the Druidic order and wrote a poem about Y Maen Chwyf:

As the sun, so shy, speeds on to hide behind the western hills
I stand within this
Ancient circle with its rugged stones
Pointing to the sky

It is possible to move the Rocking Stone by hand, which may have led to the belief that the ancient Druids performed miracles and human sacrifice here. There seems no evidence for either idea. However, it was a fitting place for Price and his fellow Neo-Druids to gather. Price's character was a mixture of fantasy and humanity, and his fertile mind conceived an idea for a Druidical museum, as well as the practical thought of using any funds raised by the museum to help the poor.

In 1839 the Chartists in Newport, northeast of Cardiff, rose in armed rebellion and the military crushed them; Price escaped to France and for some reason believed a long-forgotten prophesy that predicted Wales would be a free and independent nation. With the dust from the 1839 rising settled, Price returned once more to Wales. He became a leader of the neo-Druid movement, dressing in what he believed were authentic Druid costumes.

Despite his diversion into Druidism, Price retained his interest in democracy and hoped for equal rights for all men, not just the upper tiers of society. He was also a vegetarian decades before such a thing became fashionable, and thought that marriage was just a form of female slavery. Price also quaffed champagne as if it was water and was interested in cremation. When his son died in 1884, Price cremated him. As some considered such an act to be illegal, Price was arrested. At his trial, he proved that nothing in law specifically denied cremation and he won his case. So we have a Neo-Druid vegetarian who drank champagne rather than tea or beer and a man who chose to wear fox pelts on his head and who was against marriage. As if that was not strange enough, he also took to racing over the hills around Pontypridd stark naked – not an edifying sight in the Victorian period and undoubtedly one to scare the horses.

In 1893 Price died and an estimated 20,000 people watched his cremation, with two tons of good Welsh coal used to start him off. Not long after his smoke spiralled skyward, his loving wife decided she no longer wished to be a Druid and married the local road inspector. Price's legacy remains, however, in the Neo-Druids and in the form of a statue in Llantrisant in Glamorgan. He is fondly remembered for his eccentricities, which were many, his humanity, which was genuine, and his efforts to revive Druidism. Today Price and Anglesey are both thought of as fountains of Druidism, real or imagined.

Chapter Nine
Welsh Witches

On two occasions in my life, I have worked beside a self-confessed witch. One claimed to be a white witch and spoke about attending covens. The other followed the left-hand path, and her conversations were a great deal darker. Were they genuine witches? The white witch believed she was authentic and acted in accordance with her professed religion. The dark witch I am less sure about. I was young at the time, and it is possible she was creating an image to impress or more likely tease her immature work-mate. And that is the trouble with all of witchcraft, sorting the wheat from the chaff, the real from the imaginary, what people believe and what has only been made up and stuck under the generic label of witchcraft.

It is possible that every country in Europe has had its share of witches and Wales is no exception. If King Arthur's Merlin was born in Carmarthen, as legend claims, then he may qualify as being the most famous Welsh witch of all – unless he was a Druid- but there are others to follow his example. There was Ceridwen, for example, the mother of Taliesin the Dark Age poet. After she gave birth, Ceridwen placed Taliesin in a reed basket and launched him into the River Dovey, where Prince Elphin found him, which is a strangely familiar story. Are these stories generic across the world? Is there a common source that people learned aeons ago and carried with them during the thousands of years of folk-wandering, or did the Welsh story-tellers copy the Bible?

In more modern times, Welsh witches seem to have been much the same as in other countries but perhaps because Welsh witches were deemed useful, healers rather than users of black magic, there were fewer witch executions in Wales than elsewhere. In saying that, folklore does speak of a 16th-century witch being burned at the stake in Dolgellau in Gwynedd.

In common with most of Europe, Wales had three types of witches. Some were black witches were often associated with the devil and who cursed people and could raise the dead. Some were white witches removed curses, healed the sick and created love potions, and thirdly there were the wise men that were similar to the white witches. Merlin may have been one of the latter.

In Wales, protection against witches seems to be the same as protection against fairies. Cold iron, as in the form of a horseshoe was useful, as were branches of rowan wood or yew from outside a church, with broom also sometimes used. It is a question if these woods were sacred to Druids, and if so, perhaps the witch-beliefs are an adulterated memory of Druidic practices.

It is unlikely if any of these preventative methods would have deterred Canrig Bwt, a cannibal witch of the Dark Ages. Legend claims that Canrig Bwt lived beside an ancient cromlech at Pont-y-Cromlech on the Llanberis pass in Snowdonia and had obtained her magical powers in exchange for selling her soul to the devil. She was obviously an unpleasant woman who, according to local folklore, had a diet of raw children.

Naturally, nobody wished such a creature to haunt the countryside, but equally, nobody dared to try to kill her. However, once Canrig Bwt's ravages had grown more than people could bear one brave young man named Idwal volunteered to try and end her murders. The idea was popular, but Idwal had no experience in witch-killing so cast around for any advice that might be helpful. He was quite downcast when a local white witch told him that he needed an iron sword to kill

Canrig Bwt, for such weapons were very expensive. Idwal was about to give up the whole crazy idea of becoming a hero when a local lord loaned him his sword and threw in some close-combat lessons into the bargain.

Sword-fighting is not a skill that one can learn overnight, particularly when one has never held a sword in one's life. However, Idwal persevered, and after a few lessons, he thought he was ready. Seeing that Idwal was in earnest, others came to help, with a local wise woman advising him to cover the sword hilt with sprigs of yew and vervain. Yew was supposedly one of the Druid's magical plants while vervain is renowned as the 'herb of the cross' and has amazing medicinal properties. A monk further strengthened the sword with a blessing, dabbed Idwal's head with holy oil and absolved him of any sin if he succeeded in killing the witch.

With Idwal now fully prepared spiritually and physically, a crowd gathered to watch him march off to battle. Most well-wishers did not expect him to return but cheered anyway. After all, a forlorn hope was better than no hope at all. It was late on a dark and windy evening as Idwal grasped his sword and marched away, which seems a strange time to hunt a witch. On either side, the mountains rose stark, grim and dangerous. The moon was up when Idwal reached the cromlech and heard Canrig moving around below, grumbling and crunching at an unfortunate infant. Idwal saw the recently-gnawed bones of her latest meals.

'Canrig Bwt, you witch and eater of children; in the name of the Holy Trinity come and fight me!'

Canrig Bwt replied with a laugh that chilled Idwal's blood, saying she would suck the brain from a child and then emerge. 'And when I come out, I will kill you.' Idwal had not long to wait before the witch crawled from her den under the cromlech. She attacked Idwal at once, using her long claws to slash at him.

Idwal hefted his sword and said: 'God help me to overcome evil.'

The Lord did just that as Idwal's holy sprigs and the blessed iron sword that all witches feared halted Canrig Bwt so she could not move. Paralysed, the witch was helpless as Idwal lifted his sword and chopped off her head. The witch of Snowdonia was dead, and children were safe.

Now, is this a half-forgotten true story about a local man killing an ancient cannibal? Or is it just made up? Some elements ring true, such as blessing the sword and the use of sacred plants. One wonders how back the story goes, and if people in the 17th century substituted the word 'witch' for some other term. It is doubtful if we will ever know.

In the 16th and 17th century a witch-hunting craze settled over Europe and an estimated 100,000 people were executed in various horrible ways. Most were women. While Scotland and England were both heavily involved in witch hunting, Wales was relatively quiet with only a handful of witches or supposed witches being executed. Language may have something to do with the dearth of witch-killing, for the anti-witch treatises were never published in Welsh. The medium for witch hunting in the British Isles was English, and wherever the English language faded, fear and persecution of witches seems to have been equally limited.

However, even in Wales, some witches used the dark side, such as the 16th century Tangwlst ferch (ferch means 'daughter of') Glyn, who apparently made an idol of the Bishop of St David's and cursed him after the bishop accused her of immorality. Strangely enough, the bishop rapidly became sick...

Although King James VI and I is often blamed for the assault on witchcraft, it became a capital offence in 1563, decades before the man known somewhat oxymoronically as the Wisest Fool in Christendom became monarch of Wales and England. The first recorded execution for witchcraft in Wales was in 1594, ironically in the reign of Good Queen Bess, with Gwen ferch Ellis as the unfortunate victim. Born in Llandyrnog in the Vale of Clwyd, Gwen was brought up at Yale, not far from Wrexham. A weaver, Gwen was also a healer and a herbalist and a Christian whose folk incantations began: 'In the names of the father, the son and the Holy Ghost.' Unfortunate in her marriages, Gwen buried two husbands before she married a miller from Betws yn Rhos in Conwy.

By now Gwen was locally famous for her spells and healing, and people of all classes sought her help. One was Jane Conwy of Marl Hall. Now Jane had an affair with a man named Thomas Mostyn; Gwen found out and within a short while was accused of witchcraft. At her trial, Gwen freely admitted that she was a healer for both people and animals and had used charms to heal the sick and protect against evil. One of her charms was found to be written backwards, which was taken as a negative rather than a positive. According to the prosecution, Gwen was renowned for lifting curses that had apparently been placed on people or cattle. After she had been paid, Gwen would look into a special glass – possibly a crystal – and see where the 'cursing-pot' was located. She was known as a white witch but agreed to turn to the other side and curse Sir Thomas Mostyn. The woman who asked her to take the left-hand path was Jane Conway, whose affair with Mostyn must have turned sour.

Given such damning evidence, it was not surprising that witnesses spoke against Gwen, saying she was a nasty woman who had murdered a sick man and caused a child to go mad. Found guilty, the authorities hanged Gwen in Denbigh that same year. She claimed that she was innocent right to the end. Conway, the possible instigator, escaped. In most other countries, such an example might have led to a plethora of accusation and executions. Wales did not follow the contemporary trend.

In saying that, Wales, in common with every other nation in the British Isles, had her quota of witches. Some were avoided, and others used their power to make a living. The anti-witchcraft laws existed until 1736, but the belief in the power of witchcraft lingered in Wales well into the 19th century and, indeed, still exists today. In 1872 the Honourable W. O Stanley MP spoke of a belief in witchcraft in Anglesey. He mentioned that one of his labourers, Edward Morris, was working in Penrhos Bradwn farm when he had to remove an earthen bank. In the middle of the bank, he found 'a black pipkin with a slate covering the mouth.' The name Nanney Roberts was written on both sides of the slate while the bones of a frog were inside the pipkin with forty large pins thrust through the skin. A pipkin for those who do not know (I had to ask my wife) was an earthenware cooking pot. According to Stanley, it was a tradition to witch or curse somebody by sticking pins through a frog, attach the victim's name and hide the whole lot inside a pipkin. The curse remained intact until the person who had been witched found the pipkin. If the person performing the witching was really vindictive, he or she could burn the frog, so the curse lasted forever.

Another method of cursing was to stick pins in the frog and throw it into a pool of water to slowly drown. Apparently, girls used this form of witching against other young women who are attracted to their sweethearts. It must have been hard for frogs in parts of old Wales.

Another belief in Anglesey and possibly elsewhere in North Wales was that wells that overflowed to the south could be used as a cursing or curing well. A well near Penrhoe was often used to try and cure cancer. A man or woman who believed he or she had cancer had to wash in the water and then circle the well, dropping pins and cursing the disease. Eventually, so many people came to the well and caused so much damage to the nearby farm property that the farmer drained the well. Other wells with magical qualities were Llanailian and Holywell in Anglesey. At Llanailian, the sick person had to bathe in the well and then place alms in a chest within the local church. The chest was said to be large, heavy and studded with nails. Eventually, it was filled with coins, and the church parishioners used the money to buy three farms. One wonders if the parishioners merely used the reputation of the well for their personal advantage.

But that is to veer away from witchcraft and onto other beliefs.

One aspect of witchcraft that lingered at least until the end of the 19th century was a belief in the evil eye, and not only in the remote countryside. There was one case in Gower in the early 1860s when two men courted the same woman. Naturally, the lucky woman could just have one husband, so chose her favourite and married him. However, as soon as he was married, the husband began to suffer from asthma. When his wife was away seeing her mother, the man's asthma vanished, and he was right as rain. When his wife returned, he was again stricken by the disease. The man believed that his erstwhile love rival had hired a witch to put the evil eye on him.

Leaving his job in Gower, the stricken man moved to Swansea and searched for a 'witch curer' to remove the curse. Eventually, he found a woman who accepted his payment and said she could cure him within five months and added that after four months she would bring him the witch who had cast the curse on his house. Sure enough, the man found his condition gradually easing and when the supposed witch arrived, the house was full of friends and family, including the afflicted man's mother.

Without a qualm at being blamed for causing so much suffering and heartache, the witch agreed to lift the curse. Rather than target the man, she selected the mother as her victim and made her perform various undignified acts that were not at all suitable for a woman of her years. Once that was done the witch returned to Gower.

Was the evil eye lifted? Unfortunately, I could not find out. The man reported that he was getting better every day, but I could not locate any end result. It was a strange case for the period and one that shows the power of belief in witches even at that date. It was even stranger that although the case was reported fairly extensively in contemporary newspapers, no names were given.

Even later, in August of 1889, there was a case in Aberystwyth. An elderly woman received parish relief – a form of social security – but her neighbours were not happy with her at all. The woman was reputed to have the power of the evil eye and had the habit of staying up all night, keeping two lamps burning as she waited for a ghost she thought was haunting her. It is interesting that the neighbours did not complain about her supposed powers. Rather they were concerned that she might set the house on fire with her lamps.

When the local policeman called, he advised the lady in question to douse the lamps at night in case she fell asleep and caused a fire. The old woman refused, so the Guardians of the Workhouse stopped her parish relief and threatened to take her into the Workhouse unless she stopped looking for the ghost.

The woman succumbed to the threat and remained decently in her night-time bed after that. However, there was nearly a sting in the tail. As soon as they realised the old lady was behaving, her neighbours asked that her relief money should be reinstated. Some of the Guardians disagreed, saying that 'the belief in witchcraft is widespread and we ought to stop it by putting the woman in the workhouse.' There was heated debate before the relieving officer, who had visited the woman, said that she was 'well behaved' and ordered the parish relief to continue. It is a question which was the greater evil: the threat of witchcraft or the loathing of the Workhouse.

For those who do not know, the Workhouse was often a place of last resort. People with no income and no hope were admitted and lived a life of unremitting toil for little food. Workhouses were usually clean and sheltered but were seen as a degrading and fearful place, a dark shadow over the poverty of old age.

Today it is believed that there are numerous witches and covens in Wales and even a fair number of Satanists. Some witches are said to advertise their services quite openly. There was a curse recorded near Aberaeron in 1994, and the evil eye is not unknown. There was even a case where a new-born baby and its mother were suddenly afflicted with breathlessness after being subjected to the evil eye – similar to the case mentioned above. Perhaps there is something in the old stories after all, and the beliefs are not strange, but a natural fear of powers of body or mind that most of us do not understand. Strange Jack certainly will walk wide of any such thing.

Chapter Ten
The Miners

Mining in Wales is ancient. Near Llandudno on the north coast of the country is the Great Orme Copper Mine, which at 4,000 years old, is reputed to be the largest prehistoric mine anywhere. So when the Romans began to mine, they were tapping into a well-established practice. The Romans dug for lead and gold, with a known Roman gold mine at Dolaucothi near Pumpsaint in the Cothi Valley, Carmarthenshire. These ancient miners used both open-case and gallery mining, using a timber water-wheel to drain the galleries. When the Roman Empire recoiled in the 5th century, mining ceased for a while, only to restart around the 16th century. By the 18th, silver mining had begun at Cwmystwyth in Ceredigion, not far from the Devil's Bridge.

Despite possessing a variety of minerals, Wales is best renowned for her coal mines, with the 19th and 20th centuries being her period of peak production. Naturally, when men are confined underground in cramped and dangerous working conditions, there are rumours of strange things happening. Welsh miners, in common with miners elsewhere, have experienced many supernatural occurrences. Most are fleeting and unexplained, even today.

Arguably the most easily recognised mining area in Wales, the Rhondda is in the south of the country and comprises two valleys, the Rhondda Fach and the Rhondda Fawr, and has a number of towns including Maerdy, Tonypandy, Ferndale and Treorchy. The mining peaked before 1940 and declined after that.

The late 1860s and early 1870s seem to have been a prime time for colliery hauntings, with various unearthly noises heard deep in the pits and skeletons seen in the stalls of abandoned mines. In the closing decades of the 19th century, some ghosts were observed in the workings of the Rhondda. The Aberdare district was severely affected, with men leaving the pits, scared by the strange noises that, they swore, were never human in origin. The men were so afraid that they often refused to return to the pits until a thorough investigation had been carried out. More sceptical than the men, the mine managers descended the pits with loud voices and lanterns. On one occasion they were proved right when they shone a light into the stall where the noise had been heard and found - a cat.

Welsh miners often kept cats underground, usually in the same stalls as the pit ponies lived. If the cat wandered around and got lost in the labyrinth of working and abandoned tunnels underground, it would howl for help, and such a sound would be distorted by the constricting tunnels and passages. That was the theory the managers put forward in this instance. They may have been correct, yet there were far too many strange occurrences, seen and heard by far too many people over a long stretch of time, for cats to be the sole culprits.

For example here is an undated story that may have occurred in the early Victorian period. There is an area of South Wales known as the Heads of the Valley, with the nearest towns being Fochriw, Rhymney and Dowlais. This area had long been a centre of mining. Naturally, there were scores of old abandoned mine workings underground, at different levels, with many not adequately documented. Mines were dug in this area for ironstone as well as coal. It may have been when the Dowlais Iron Company sunk three deep water balance pits at Cwym Bargoed in 1839 that the following incident occurred.

The new workings thrust a road through the rock, with the men toiling away with pick and shovel in those days before any mechanical aids. After a while, the hard heading of the new road broke into the road of another mine, and all work stopped for a while. The rippers, the men who were removing the rock above the seam and raised the height of the road, stopped, worried about possible gas or a rush of flood water. Neither evil occurred, so two of the rippers pushed through into the newly discovered mine. Holding their lamps high, they stepped cautiously forward and saw the dim shape of another miner sitting on the ground further along the road.

'Halloa,' the rippers shouted, wondering if they had accidentally entered the level of a working mine.

The man did not reply. He continued to sit still and silent. The rippers walked up to him. 'He's asleep on the job,' one said and put out a hand to wake him. At one touch, the strange miner dissolved into dust. Both rippers jumped back and ran to their own shaft. They found out later that the body had belonged to a miner who had died half a century before, trapped underground by a rock fall.

What may be a variation of that story was dated to 1870, a time that the Vochriw coal pits of the Dowlais Iron Company already had a strange reputation. In July that year the men were pumping water from one of the old pits to deepen the shaft, and at the bottom, they found the skeleton of a human male, with a heavy chain attached to a tram wheel. They thought it was the remains of a labourer named Richard Jones, who disappeared in 1859.

Other miners had less tangible but possibly more supernatural encounters.

In September 1887 seven colliers at the Ocean Colliery at Cwnpark in the Rhondda were walking to the coal face when something tapped the last man on the shoulder. He turned around and saw a female, who promptly vanished. The man told his comrades, and they were immediately spooked and ran out of the pit. The woman appeared again and jumped on the shoulders of one of the men before vanishing a second time. There is not even an attempted explanation for that particularly strange encounter.

Clyncorrwg Colliery beside Port Talbot in Glamorgan had some strange encounters when a group of miners believed that they saw a ghost and refused to return to the pit. Within an hour or so 300 miners were on strike. One may ask why miners were so easily scared. It was a common belief that such sightings were warnings of an impending disaster.

In July 1902 the men reported seeing a ghostly woman walking the tunnels and waving a lantern down the Clyncorrwg pit. As women did not work underground, that was impossible. Furthermore, other men claimed to have heard the woman screaming, the rumble of a rock fall and pleas for help. Others had seen flashes of light. Rather than believe they had seen a spectre from the past, the miners thought they had seen a vision from the future. They thought there would soon be some significant calamity, possibly flooding from a nearby abandoned mine.

It is possible to scoff at such things from the comfort of a centrally-heated 21st-century house. Put yourself in a dark pit hundreds of feet underground, and your point of view might alter very quickly. Now think of the known 152 mining disasters in Wales, and these were only the incidents that led to multiple fatalities, not the ordinary day-to-day dangers. The men working down the pits were not cowards; they understood the risks and warnings far more than we could ever do.

The colliers had other premonitions of doom. For instance in October 1913 at Senghenydd Colliery in Glamorgan, a robin, dove and pigeon fluttered around the pithead, which the miners thought foretold a calamity. Sure enough, later that day a terrible explosion killed 439 men.

Sometimes the premonition of mine workers stopped all work and led to serious meetings at a high level. In July 1902, 43 Union delegates who represented 10,000 miners held their monthly meeting at the Hotel Metropole in Swansea. At the meeting, they discussed a stoppage at Clyncorrwg Colliery in Glamorgan 'on account of superstitious worries'. The local MP, Brynmor Jones had become involved and visited the Home Office, and officials searched plans of old workings in the area to check for any possible danger from disused pits with gas or flooding. Rather than mocking the men, the delegates said that the opinion of old and experienced miners should be respected.

One of the worst disasters in Wales and the most poignant occurred at Aberfan on the 21st October 1966 when a mining spoil tip slid onto Pantglas Junior School and other buildings, with 116 children and 28 adults killed. As many as 200 people had predicted the horror in one way or another.

In the 19th century, Morfa Colliery at Port Talbot earned an unenviable reputation and became known as the Pit of Ghosts. In 1863 the mine was plagued with strange sightings and rumours of ghosts. One particular sighting was of a dog, the 'red dog of Morfa' that appeared and then vanished. That same year, after the sightings, an explosion killed 40 men. Sightings of the Red Dog continued, and in February 1870 another explosion killed a further 29 men. Sometimes miners just seemed to sense when something was wrong. In 1890 the colliers in Morfa smelled something different. They did not know what it was but knew it was not right. They claimed the scent was sweet, a perfume like roses, and believed that said it came from unseen 'death flowers', possibly linked to the flowers laid on coffins or graves. On the 10th March, that year about half the morning shift were spooked by the smell and the sound of voices where nobody was working. They also heard noises they described as 'like thunder in the distance and the slamming of air-doors' and visions of what they thought were spirits at the foot of the Cribbwr vein. Men were justifiably scared, given the history of the place, and left the pit, preferring to work in neighbouring Maesteg. By not turning up for work, they broke their working contract and left themselves open to all sorts of disciplinary action. However, the colliers were proved correct when later that day they heard a massive explosion and 87 men were buried alive. Morfa certainly earned its unpleasant reputation.

Even after the 1890 disaster, tales of ghosts and strange happenings continued with knockings and wailings heard underground as well as muffled drums and male voices singing dirges. An investigation that year found that there were an estimated six 'restless spirits' who were taken to be the spirits of men who died in one of the mine's explosions.

The mine is shut now, but the ghosts may still remain.

In 1904, Brace's Level at Pontypool was said to be haunted by the ghost of a man with a light in the centre of his forehead. The figure was reported to be tapping the roofs and sides of the Meadow Vein. At that time the mining company, Baldwin Ltd had recently re-opened workings that had been closed 150 years previously, and the men were naturally concerned about safety. When the miners saw the strange figure, they turned and ran, with some claiming they had also heard groans coming from the long-abandoned workings. A few men refused to work alone at the Meadow Vein or in the old workings, particularly as the man with the light could only be seen from one direction. The light in the forehead sounds suspiciously like a collier wearing a miner's helmet, which was not compulsory until the middle of the 20th century. A vision of the future, perhaps?

Cwm Colliery in South Wales was also said to be haunted by the ghost of an old miner who walked through a sandbagged wall into old deserted workings. According to folklore, the ghost was of an ironman from Tonypandy who had been squashed by minecars. Mining was always incredibly dangerous, even in the 20th century.

When there was a fatal accident in mine, all work ended for the day or until after the funeral. Some miners believed that the spirit of a man killed in the pit remained there until he was properly buried and perhaps they are correct.

Miners lived in a world unlike any other. Underground, with little daylight and only dim lamp-light, in constant danger of gas, fire, flooding or cave-ins, they were a community apart. Before science explained fire-damp and gas, or the natural movement of rocks underground, any sounds could be interpreted as *coblyns*, small creatures that were believed to infest the mines, while fires could have been caused by the fiery gaze of basilisks.

The name coblyns otherwise known as *bwca* seems to mean both sprite or knocker. The bwca is a small creature, like a miniature miner dressed in mining gear and they live underground in the pits, whether working or abandoned. Apparently, they are not unfriendly, although they can be mischievous, moving things around and pinching anything they can get their hands on. It has been said that they don't actually exist and miners only imagined them, although some serious-minded people thought the knocking noise they made was the creaking and groaning of timbers underground before a rock fall or cave in. Other miners, who knew the creatures better, believed the bwca made the noises to warn their human companions that a cave-in threatened. Old miners did not scoff at bwca, otherwise known as Tommy knockers. The old miners sometimes believed that the dead remained to haunt the mines, with the spirit coming back to the old haunts of the body. Sometimes the bwca drills, sometimes it runs a phantom car or wanders through the old workings or knocks to warn of danger.

When Welsh miners emigrated to the United States, they took the bwca with them. Sometimes the bwca appeared outside the mines, where they continued with their love of occasionally dangerous practical jokes. They have also been known to act as guides to unwary travellers, leading them to a cliff edge by candlelight before blowing out the candle and running away, laughing at the fun of watching a human tottering on the brink of death. They also have bad tempers, so it is better to praise them than not. And if you are blessed with a long nose, or if you are teetotal, avoid them for they have no time for you.

There is the well-known tale of the bwca in Monmouthshire who worked on a farm for the usual payment of a bowl of milk. When the farm servant substituted urine for milk, the bwca boxed her ears and shifted home to a nearby farm, where the servant asked his name. The bwca refused to give it, so the servant listened as he gloated over his reticence in a song, where he mentioned his name. Immediately in a huff, the bwca left, to work in a third farm where he struck up a friendship with a servant named Moses. Unfortunately, Moses became involved in the Wars of the Roses. When Moses died in battle, the bwca was so hurt he became malicious, and the farmer sought professional help. A local wise man grabbed the bwca by his nose and sent him to the Red Sea for 14 generations. His time must surely be up now.

But that is to meander a long way from haunted mines. Even in the 20th century, Welsh miners could have uncanny experiences. At

Taff Merhyr the mine managers recorded that 'unearthly sightings' had been observed, while in Abercynon colliery an electrician saw a light moving along the level toward him. Believing it was somebody checking on the work he continued working on a panel until the man came close. To his horror, it was a man who had died five years before. Dropping his tools, the electrician ran until he reached the pit bottom and refused to ever work alone in that section of the pit again.

As recently as the 1980s, people have seen a couple of phantom miners in the Llechwedd Slate Caverns at Blaenau Ffestiniog in Gwynedd, while the sounds of men working have also been heard. Also in the 1980s in Dylife in Powys, a man was walking through the disused mine tunnels when he saw a blue light about five feet tall, in front of him. The light moved as he moved. Such sights were not unknown in the mines where miners often saw lights floating in the tunnel and then soaring into the sky. On a more sinister note, one day a body of miners at Maesteg in Mid Glamorgan were playing cards when a stranger joined them. The miners grew suspicious when the stranger won all the games, and then they noticed his cloven feet and fled. The devil evidently had decided to return to Wales after his humiliation at the Devil's Bridge.

Naturally, an industry with such a long history boasted created a plethora of other superstitious. For example, if a miner met a woman with a squint while he was on his way to the pit, he would immediately turn around and go home. In South Wales, miners would not start any new job on a Friday – which is a day that mariners also held to be unlucky. On Good Friday, many pits were deserted. At home, miners' wives would place the family cat in a cold oven and hang the coal-tongs from the mantel to bring good luck. Naturally, such beliefs were not confined to coal mines. For instance, in 1878 the quarrymen at Penrhyn in Gwynedd refused to work on Ascension Day in case it caused an accident. There was a reason: when the local agent forced the men to work earlier in the century, there was a spate of casualties.

The miners also had their own code of conduct that glued them together and kept working conditions as safe and decent as possible.

Men were expected to keep to the code, and if they broke it, they were not popular. One crime was the fraudulent marking of loaded trams. When discovered, the fraudster who had probably marked the trams of several men was grabbed and taken to the cage and hauled up to the surface. All the miners would gather around him and cover him with flour, a white man amongst his coal-black colleagues.

In that state, he was then thrust to the forefront of the men who followed in a long procession and marched through the streets of his mining town. Each man would point to him without saying a word. The fraudster would be taken home in that condition, degraded and would soon leave the district.

Today, the mining industry in Wales is less than a shadow of what it once was. However, the memories remain, with the National Mining Memorial commemorating the disasters at the site of the Universal Colliery Disaster in Senghenydd. There are also various mining museums remembering the hard and dangerous lives of the miners. These men and their women deserve to be recognised.

I must admit that I did not enjoy researching or writing that chapter. I remember the Aberfan disaster and the grief it caused. I also have generations of miners in my ancestry and can empathise with the men in the pits and the women who worried about them. There is no doubt that the miners were a community apart and I take my hat off to them.

Chapter Eleven
Legends of Llangynwyd

Llangynwyd in the Llynvi Valley is a cosy little village in the south of Wales, two miles south of Maesteg. On the surface, it appears a bustling, friendly place, but underneath, the community is seething with a plethora of legends. One of the best known is the story of the Maid of Cefn Ydfa. According to the tradition, the Maid was Ann Thomas, who was born in 1704 and was forced to marry a man she did not love.

Ann's father gave her as a ward to a local lawyer named Anthony Maddocks. In the early 18th century young women had few rights, and when Maddocks ordered Ann to marry his son, she had no choice but to obey. However, rather than the wealthy Maddocks boy, Ann loved a thatcher and poet named Will Hopcyn. When Maddocks senior found out about Ann's sweetheart, he was furious. He banned Ann from meeting Hopcyn and locked her in her room, like a naughty child. However, love will out, and Ann found a friendly servant who agreed to carry love letters from Ann to Hopcyn and back. Between the three they had a regular arrangement with an oak tree being used as an impromptu post office.

For a while everything went well, the two lovers communicated and passed messages of undying love back and forth, and then Maddocks' wife, and Ann's future mother-in-law found out. She was not happy about her son's soon-to-be wife having an affair and stripped Ann's room of paper and ink and anything else that could be used to create a message. Ann refused to be defeated. Rather than give way to despair, she opened her window, leaned outside and plucked leaves from the nearest tree. The leaves she used for paper, and she cut into her arm to use blood as ink.

Unfortunately, the story does not have a happy ending. The Maddocks family forced Ann to the altar, and she eventually said 'I do' to a man she did not love. Unable to stand seeing his love with somebody else, Hopcyn left the area. Ann wasted away, and as she neared death, she asked for her lover; Hopcyn rushed to be with her, and she died in his arms. Ann was buried in St Cynwyd's Church.

As well as that strange love story, the locals have the advantage of The Old House, founded in 1147 and one of the oldest pubs in Wales, which itself is worthy of a mention. At the time of writing, I am not certain that it is operating, although I hope it is. Patrons have included Richard Burton and David Bowie while Ann Romney, wife of the United States Republican presidential candidate Mitt Romney spent an entire day here. Ann Romney's Welsh connections are strong as her grandfather was David Davies, a Nantyffyllon coalminer who immigrated to the USA in the 1920s. Other watering-holes dispute that the Old House is the oldest pub, with the Skirrid Inn near Abergavenny claiming to have been serving drinks since 1110. The Blue Anchor at Aberthaw could possibly date to 1130, and there are others, for Wales has a long history of conviviality as well as some strange customs.

Few are strangers than Llangynwyd's ancient folk custom of Mary Lwyd. This wassailing ceremony possibly predates Christianity although it was not recorded until 1800. Essentially the ceremony was a procession through the village headed by a horse's skull on a pole. A gang of men carried the horse's head and sing their way from house to house. As there are more details of this custom elsewhere in the book, that is all I shall say for now.

Near to the village, there is an ancient castle, Llangynwyd Castle, which gives some historical significance to the tales.

According to local lore, Llangynwyd Castle contains a hidden chest of gold with, of course, a spiritual guardian. This watchman ensures that nobody will ever find the treasure by leaving them confused and lost. There is also an underground passage from the castle all the way to the nearby village, although, despite many searches, nobody has yet been able to find it. It is entirely possible that there was an underground passage, of course, usually a safe route to water or an escape route if things got tough.

In common with most Welsh castles, Llangynwyd had its share of battle. It was attacked in 1257 and destroyed in 1293. It is now a ruin, as are many genuine ancient castles, and is situated in a pretty position at the head of a small valley with ferns and tall trees. And then in 1902 the ghost stories started. The first ghost was that of a tall nun, seen strolling from Maesteg, solemn-faced and demure. She passed the pine trees, crossed the valley and the moat of the castle and floated over the ruins as if walking on air or following some ancient path and staircase that no longer exists. After standing on the highest point of the ruins, she vanished.

Once the news spread, the local people came to see this ghost. Some would have been believers, but most were cynics, hoping to unveil a hoaxer. It was a farmer who was next to see the nun, and he set his dog on her. He could not believe it when, as he watched, the nun transmogrified into a colossal rabbit 'as big as sheep' that terrified the dog into running back to its master. The farmer, sensible man, withdrew; a rabbit as big as a sheep would be something to avoid.

Other would-be ghost hunters continued to be curious. One man saw the nun on all fours, 'scratching' at the ruins with her bare hands, possibly searching for the treasure, which is a strange thing for a ghost to do. Perhaps that same watcher summoned his friends, for shortly afterwards a group of men surrounded the castle and crept up on it. The nun was there, but as the men approached she again turned into a hare and jinked between them to escape.

It was well known that witches have the power to transform themselves into hares, so perhaps there is a connection? Whether the ghost is truth or fiction, Llangynwyd Castle, like the village, is well worth a visit.

Chapter Twelve
Enchanting Islands

Perhaps the most magical part of Wales is her coastline and the islands offshore. Each of these scraps of land has its quota of strange stories, legends and myths. Some are believable, some less so and others one can only smile at, while still enjoying the work of the original story-teller who fabricated a tale out of shady beliefs and whispered folklore.

To stand on the western coast of Wales and look out to sea is to experience beauty. Even on the dullest day when the skies glower down and the waves thunder against the cliffs, there is something special about this place. Western Wales is like nowhere else, and one reason for that is the Magical Islands. I had not heard about the Magical Islands until I arrived in Pembrokeshire and I still have not seen them. Not even Mrs Prichard, for all her local lore, could honestly say that she has been there. She told me that their other name is the Green Meadows of Enchantment and said that only the fortunate few can visit them, and then only briefly. I was not one of that number; perhaps one day I will meet somebody who is.

In Scotland, the land of Tir-nan-Og was said to lie somewhere to the west, and in Celtic mythology there was Avalon. Perhaps these islands off Pembrokeshire are one and the same, shifting with the tide or the population movements during the Folk Wandering of the Dark Ages. I was told by a solemn-faced, twinkling-eyed local worthy that

St David's Head is the best place to view these islands. As the rain was sleeting down on my first visit and visibility was about fifty yards, I did not have much luck.

According to folklore, some of the old-time sailors actually landed on these magical islands, but once they returned to their ships, the islands vanished as if they had never been. I have had that experience on the islands of the Scottish west coast when the fog closed in, so perhaps there was a good reason that has nothing to do with magic. Or maybe not.

These islands seem to have similar properties to the fairy mounds and hills that bless the countryside. People who land spend what they believe to be a few delightful hours, only to find that when they leave, years have passed. One version of the many legends claims that the islands were home to a good-looking race known as the *Plant Rhys Ddwfn*, the Children of Rhys of the Deep. At one time these ethereal people eased across to the mainland to shop at the markets in Laugharne and Milford Haven. They were seldom seen, except by those with the power of second sight, but they did not exploit their invisibility, paying for everything they purchased.

According to legend, these Magical Islands were not naturally invisible. The Children of Rhys were amazing gardeners who grew special herbs that hid the islands. The herbs were virtually unknown on the mainland, growing only in one area on St David's Head. One version of the story claimed that if anybody plucked or stepped on the herbs, she or he could see the enchanted islands. That is what happened to a man named Gruffydd ab Einion, who stumbled on the herbs by mistake and the next day saw the islands. He sailed out and – saw nothing. The islands had vanished. For a while Gruffydd was disconsolate, and then had the idea of returning to St David's Head and lifting some of the herbs.

That ploy worked, and the next time Gruffydd put to sea the islands were visible in all their glory. He landed, to find the Children of Rhys friendly and hospitable, although they asked him to hand over the herbs he had cut. As soon as he complied, they smiled and granted him gold and treasures that set him up for life.

I did try to find that patch of herbs on St David's Head. Anybody watching must have thought me very strange as I walked back and forth – and they were undoubtedly right. Nobody is as Strange as Jack. Anyway, I did not find the herbs, although I would not have recognised them if I had. Better luck next time, perhaps. I will not write what my wife called me during my search: some things are best left unsaid and anyway, young people may read this book.

One island on which it is possible to land is Grassholm, which is home to a colony of gannets. Of course, this being Wales where everything has a story, this noisy lump of rock has a legend attached to it. If the old people are correct, then this islet used to be known as Gwales. *The Mabinogion* mentions Gwales as the location for the Assembly of the Wondrous Head.

Back in the old pre-Christian days, the Gods of Britain and the Gods of Ireland were not the best of friends. During a British raid on Ireland, the Irish gods decapitated a British giant-god named Bran. Despite having nothing beneath his neck, Bran instructed his men to carry him to London and bury him under the White Mount, to guard the country against all comers. The Assembly of British Gods travelled back over the Irish Sea to Harlech, where they feasted for seven years while harpers played great music and singers sang beautiful songs. From Harlech, they sailed to Gwales, which at that time had the most fantastic hall. The hall had three doors, but only two could be used. The third door was permanently closed, and Bran ordered that it should remain in that condition. After eighty years of feasting and drinking, one god, Heilyr, son of Gwyn could resist temptation no longer, and he opened the forbidden door. All at once all the negativity of the past including the death of Bran returned in full force. Now full of sorrow, the British gods left the island and walked to London to bury Bran's head. And there it remained until a bright young king named Arthur unearthed it centuries later. Or so the story says.

There are plenty of other islands off the coast of Wales, one of which is Caldey, which can easily be visited as there is a wee boat that takes you there from the mainland. Known as a Cradle of Celtic Christianity, the small island of Caldey lies just off the coast of Tenby in Carmarthen Bay. It is about two miles south of Giltar Point on the opposite side of Caldey Sound. As was common in Wales, a Celtic Christian community set up home here, settling in around 540, although the island's name is said to come from a Norseman named Caldeye. I wonder what it was called before that stray Norseman arrived. The Christian connection was reinforced in 1113 when Cistercian monks arrived and built a priory, which survived until 1536 when Henry VIII of Wales and England embarked on his maniacal destruction of anything Roman Catholic. Henry the Crazed must have been whirling in his grave when monks returned to the island in 1923. They are still there in spite of Henry's spleen.

Despite, or perhaps because of, the holiness of this island, it has a plethora of mystery and legend attached. For example, the old church of St Illtud holds the 6th-century Caldey Stone with an incomplete Ogham inscription that apparently commemorates a son of Dunracunas. I would like to sound smart and give a full translation but reading Ogham was not one of my best subjects at school. There is also a later Latin inscription:

Et Singnocr Crusin Illam Fingsi Rogo Omnibu Anmalantibus Ibi Exorent Pro Animae Catuoconi

That apparently reads as: 'And by the sign of the cross which I have fashioned upon this stone, I ask all who walk there that they pray for the soul of Catuocunus'.

If the combination of Latin and Ogham on this fascinating little church is not strange, then look at the floor: it is made of pebbles from the beach, while the spire is strangely twisted, a leaning tower of Caldey.

There were even some strange characters among the holy men, such as St Pyr or Piro who liked his tipple. One day he enjoyed himself so much that he fell in the well and drowned.

Much, much later, pirates are said to have used this little island. It is strange that when people talk about pirates or write about pirates, they rarely consider Wales, while Wales gave the world some of the most notorious. One of the most successful and famous, or perhaps infamous buccaneer-pirates of all time, Sir Henry Morgan was as Welsh as they come. Not many mariners could boast a career such as his, from pirating to becoming an admiral of the Royal Navy and lieutenant-governor of Jamaica. Morgan was also mentioned in the hit film *Pirates of the Caribbean* and has a brand of rum named after him; he would probably enjoy the latter claim to fame more than all the rest. His house of Penllwyn Manor in Pontllanfraith still exists. Henry Morgan is perhaps the best known, but others were equally as unpleasant to cross.

For instance, there was Howell Davis who was born in Milford Haven. He is hardly remembered, but on one occasion in 1719 he captured a slave ship off the coast of Guinea. One of the crew was Little Newcastle born Bartholomew Roberts. Recognising a fellow Welshman, Davis persuaded Roberts to turn pirate and eventually Roberts rose to fame, or notoriety, as Black Bart or *Barti Ddu*.

Black Bart was reputedly a highly organised pirate who barred rum on his ships and forbade women and boys. Women caused trouble, and as some pirates had the same sexual attraction to boys, they could also be troublesome. Bart's first foray into piracy earned him 40,000 moidores and a diamond-and-gold cross which he wore from that day until his death. The cross glittered nicely against his damask suit with the feathered cap on top. The Christian image continued when he tried to persuade a captured priest to remain on board as the ship's chaplain. Possibly sensibly, the holy man refused the position. Perhaps he looked up at Black Bart's flag and thought it less than Christian. He would have been correct, for the flag was an image of Roberts standing on two skulls, one skill marked A.B.H. – a Barbadian's Head and the other A.M.H – a Martinican's Head, doubtless as a threat to the authorities of these islands, who must have wronged Roberts in the past.

Bart is reputed to have captured over 400 ships, and then, in 1721 the Royal Navy, in the person of Captain Chaloner Ogle of HMS *Swallow* killed him off Parrot Island, on the coast of Guinea. Strangely, his townspeople, rather than being ashamed of having such a prolific wrong-doer, erected a monument on the village green.

Even less known outside Wales is Leekie Porridge. The name comes from a local delicacy, a sort of thick soup of chicken, oats and leeks. Leekie came from Tenby and in those days of shifting loyalties, served with John Paul Jones and came home to Tenby. He lived there in peace for a few years until a visiting ship-master recognised the shoes he was wearing. The shoes had distinctive silver buckles, and the captain had owned them until John Paul Jones had stolen them and passed them onto Leekie. The authorities immediately arrested Leekie and a court sentenced him to be pressed into the Royal Navy, where he served as a quartermaster until his discharge.

Wales seems to have had an ambiguous relationship with pirates, privateers, wreckers and smugglers. In the Dark Ages, Irish pirates and slave-raiders certainly haunted the coasts, and Welshmen were always quick to deal with any Norse incursions. While the Norse conquered vast tracts of what is now England and much of Western Scotland, the Welsh seem to have been much more successful in repelling the fierce warriors of the north.

Henry Morgan, that most enigmatic of buccaneers is reputed to have used Caldey as a base, although it is a long sail from his theatre of operations in the Caribbean. The Scottish-American privateer John Paul Jones is also suspected of using Caldey Island as his headquarters when his ships attacked Fishguard in 1779. According to legend, Jones died in 1792, and somebody shoved his corpse into a hole in the rocks near Ord Point on Caldey Island. Although history would argue that Jones was buried elsewhere, folklore is adamant that Jones is still on the island and can be heard digging for his buried treasure. I have always wondered why pirates and privateers went to a great deal of trouble concealing their wealth, and then promptly forgot where it was. Why not just spend it?

There was smuggling too, of course, with houses along the Welsh coast suspected of having secret tunnels. Solva in Pembrokeshire was notorious for such things. Wrecking was not unknown, and many people welcomed the bounty that a storm brought. In Wolf's Castle, also in Pembrokeshire a horn was sounded when a ship was wrecked so the locals could flock to the coast and plunder. In 1791 a vessel known as *Increase of Scarborough* came ashore at Druidston Haven in St Bride's Bay. Some accounts say that the locals helped the survivors ashore while other stories claim darker deeds of slit throats and robbed bodies. Either way, the looters found the rum store and imbibed heavily. With their senses stupefied by alcohol, they began to throw around the kegs of gunpowder the ship carried; somebody must have lit his pipe and – boom. It was a strange way for a looter to end, but satisfying to know that the ship fought back. Wrecking and looting could be a lucrative business, with some houses along the Pembrokeshire coast built on the profits of other men's misery. One man, George Llewellyn from St Davids was locally famous for creating a windmill from the proceeds of broken ships.

Smugglers are said to have hidden their good in Cathedral caves on Caldey, which also has its resident ghost, a black monk that used to frequent the priory and other parts of the island. Naturally, a story wraps around this monk. When Henry VIII was destroying the fabric of Roman Catholicism in Wales and England, the monks of Glastonbury bundled up their treasure and handed into the care of one man.

'Whatever happens,' they said. 'Make sure that Henry does not get it.'

The monk swore on the Bible that he would die rather than allow Henry to steal the church's treasure. Leaving Glastonbury, the monk travelled to Wales, aware that Henry's men were tracking him with their grasping, avaricious fingers ready to clutch all the gold of the church. Hefting his treasure, the monk escaped through the breadth of Wales and took the boat to Caldey. All the time, Henry's men were following, and eventually, the fugitive monk heard his pursuers were about to cross to the island. Remembering his vow, the monk found a quiet corner, gave a last prayer, piled up the treasure and slowly bricked himself in so the greedy king would not get his treasure. He died there, faithful to the end, and it is said that on certain nights when the moon is low, and the waves hush over the pebbly beach, those who have the power can see a golden glow around the monk's final resting place.

I tried, of course, and didn't see a damned thing. I tripped over a branch, barked my shin and nearly broke my fool neck searching for that treasure. The monk can keep it. Apparently, he was well over six foot tall and sometimes emerges from the graveyard before wandering silently around the island. Possibly he was off to talk to his ghostly chums, the white lady and the crazy man who have also been seen, but not recently.

Finally, Caldey was thought of as a sort of half-way-house for the dead. According to legend, when people died, their bodies were carried across to Caldey to ensure their spirits did not plague those they left behind.

No visit to the Welsh islands would be complete without a trip to Bardsey. Its correct name is Ynys Enlli - the Island in the Currents - which is as practical as most Celtic place names. The more romantic see the name Ynys Fenlii as coming from a legendary, or more likely mythological, Irish warrior called Benlli Gawr who invaded and sub-dued Powys. However, most non-Welsh speakers use the Anglicised version of Bardsey.

Using the English version is strange: surely the native tongue should take precedence over an imposed language in place names as in all else. I cannot imagine the French or Italians using English names for their islands. But that is to veer from our course to the island.

Bardsey is also known as the 'Island of 20,000 Saints' although I doubt they would all fit in the island at the same time. It is about two miles off the Llyn Peninsula in Gwynedd in North West Wales. As so often, the origin of the English name is disputed. Some say the island was named after a Norseman, while others believe the name means the Island of the Bards. So far, not much strange about Ynys Enlli, then, but now things get interesting. This island was Wales' own Iona, a holy island with a history that extended for thousands of years.

According to what passes for history, in the early 6th century Saint Cadfan sailed from Brittany to found St Mary's Abbey. By the seventh century as many as 2,500 monks are said to have lived on this scrap of an island, and perhaps their graves mark the 20,000 saints, for being buried here guarantees eternal salvation. It is said that in the middle ages the church claimed that three pilgrimages to Ynys Enlli equated with one to Rome, giving this windy island the nickname of the Rome of Britain.

With such a long religious history it is perhaps not surprising that Ynys Enlli was once thought to be Avalon, and is one of the reputed burial sites of King Arthur. Ynys Enlli is a bit greedy as it also claims the burial place of Merlin. Strangely enough, the most fanciful stories claim that Merlin has nine bards to keep him company as he lies in a glass tower with the Thirteen Treasures of Britain.

I don't suppose that many people know what these thirteen treasures are. Well, here they are, in no particular order:

The sword of Drnwyn, whose blade turns to fire as soon as a king holds the hilt.
Gwyddno Garanhir's hamper that increases its content by a factor of five.
The Horn of Bran that could refill itself with whatever the holder wished to drink. (Imagine that next time the Welsh rugby team win the six nations!)
The Chariot of Morgan the Wealthy, which was probably the Celtic equivalent of a magic carpet as it could go anywhere at high speed.
The Halter of Clyno Eiddyn; this was a useful little tool when horses were the ultimate in transport. The owner of the halter only had to dream of a horse, and the next morning it would be in his or her stables, neatly haltered and ready to ride.

The Cauldron of Diwrnach, which was a bit selective as it only boiled water for a man who was brave. To the Celtic people, bravery was everything.

The Knife of Llawfronedd the Horseman, which carved meat for two dozen men. Now that would be useful at Christmas.

The Whetstone of Tudwal Tudglyd, this stone was used to sharpen the blade of a warrior's sword, so it always killed, leaving none of these messy, non-fatal wounds.

The Coat of Padarn Redcoat, which fitted anyone of noble blood but nobody else. That is an interesting item that showed both the aristocratic nature of Celtic society and the importance of the colour red, which is something to bear in mind when considering the origins of the British military uniform.

The Crock of Rhygenydd, which would be a tremendously useful tool as it served whatever food was desired. Imagine a feast with no cooking.

The Chessboard of Gwenddolau. For some strange reason, this chess set played itself.

Finally, the Mantle of Arthur. Whoever wore this would be invisible, which would be very useful if the Crock of Rhygenydd served mediocre food.

These items may be strange by today's standards, but they reveal the nature of Arthur's Celtic society with its emphasis on warfare, feasting, horsemanship and nobility.

One version of the legend claims that the Lady of the Lake imprisoned Merlin in this tower; another said that he chose self-immolation together with nine bards.

As with most Celtic legends, history and mythology are intertwined with magic and fantastic fiction. It has been suggested that after the Battle of Camlann, wherever that took place, Arthur was carried to Morgan le Fay on Ynys Enlli. Morgan and her nine sisters were possibly the same nine bards who accompanied Merlin.

Now that is interesting, if mythological.

If Ynys Enlli is equated as Avalon, then we need to find another connection apart from mythology. How about apples? Avalon means the 'Island of Apples' from the Welsh *afal* or *aballon* meaning apple. It seems that one of the colonies of monks who lived on Ynys Enlli grew fruit trees and, after centuries of Norse raids, pirates, foul weather and the dissolution of the monasteries, the orchard gradually faded away. However, in 1998 a local nurseryman named Ian Sturrock discovered an ancient and much-battered apple tree on the island, beside the 13th-century abbey. The tree proved to be unique, an unrecorded variety now known as the Bardsey apple.

So then, this island grew apples. There is no glass tower though unless the long-gone monks had an early greenhouse. Merlin, either as a Druid or a monk with knowledge of herbs and fruit, might have retired to such a place. He may have taken on the life of a monk. There is another Merlin connection with the Hermit's Cave on a hillside, which is another place where Merlin is said to be buried.

On this strange island, even the lighthouse is unusual. Bardsey Lighthouse, dating from 1821, is distinctive for its red and white bands and is square, rather than the usual circular tower.

Finally, the island had its own line of kings. Presumably 'king' was the title given to the head man of the island. The last of the line was Love Pritchard, who tried to volunteer to fight the Kaiser in 1914. The War Office thought he was too old at 71 years and refused his offer, whereupon King Love announced that his realm of Bardsey was neutral and not part of the war. He was one of the few sensible rulers in that era of mass slaughter. His crown still exists and is on display in Bangor Museum.

From islands with their own king and Merlin's crystal tower to islands of pirate treasure and islands that disappear, nobody can deny that Wales' islands are anything but strange. Each one is unique in its own way, with its own atmosphere. Each one is worth a visit. Just watch for the ghosts.

Chapter Thirteen
A Gathering of Ghosts

Ghosts are strange things. Some people believe fervently in their existence, others are equally adamant that they don't exist and both sides are prepared to argue that their opinion is always right and the other side always wrong. I stand on the sidelines in these discussions and act as referee. This chapter contains some small and supposedly true occurrences of ghosts in Wales. As a departure from my usual ramblings, I have tried to introduce some order by placing each story separately, under its own sub-heading.

Mrs Phillips and her daughter

The first story is from Swansea in the south of the country, and dated 1897. The 19th century saw many waves of Christian revival, and in one of them, the Ebenezer Chapel was built in Swansea. In 1897 the chapel was located in Skinner Street and was one of the most popular and best attended Baptist chapels in Wales. Indeed it was so well known that people used the building as a landmark and a rendezvous.

That year Mrs Annie Phillips was living a few streets away, together with her teenage daughter. As anybody who has ever brought up teenagers will know, parents live in a constant state of worry for the safety of their children. That situation was amplified in the 19th century when the slightest hint of non-respectability could ruin a girl's reputation and even her future life. It is understandable that when Mrs Phillips should fret when young Margaret Phillips was consistently late home. Calling on a friend, Mrs Phillips stormed through the streets to the address Margaret had told her she was visiting.

As she passed Ebenezer Chapel, Mrs Skinner saw her daughter standing on the pavement, wearing a long grey cloak that nearly touched the ground.

'Hello, my child, you're coming home,' Mrs Phillips said, grasping her daughter firmly by the shoulder. She added a few more words of motherly advice and pulled Margaret towards her.

Or at least she tried to. As Mrs Phillips pulled, her daughter's head vanished, 'exactly like a jack in the box,' Mrs Phillips later said.

Realising that Margaret's head was too firmly attached to her body to disappear in such a manner, Mrs Phillips knew that who, or whatever, this cloaked woman might be, it was not Margaret. When the creature turned into smoke and poured through the keyhole in the chapel door, Mrs Phillips gave a small scream and clung onto her companion for support. The terrified women ran past the chapel to pick up Margaret. There appears no record of what Mrs Phillips said to her wayward daughter.

That particular ghost had appeared before. Again materialising as a female in a long cloak, it had drifted toward a young girl who was visiting a relative's grave in the graveyard. When the girl screamed and ran away, the ghost followed her, silently. Local people did not know what to make of this spectre. Most hoaxers employed long white sheets, and none of them could disappear through a keyhole. Naturally, there was speculation, with the smart money on the spirit of a woman whose grave had recently been opened in the graveyard.

Whether that was true or not, the grey-cloaked ghost seemed to like Mrs Phillips, for it appeared to her on a later occasion. Mrs Phillips was in her house when she heard a tapping on her window. She looked out, to see the ghost there.

'Go to bed, go to bed.' The ghost ordered.

As a Welshwoman and a mother, Mrs Phillips had no intention of allowing some unknown woman to tell her what to do.

'I'll give you go to bed if I come out, I tell you,' Mrs Phillips said.

The ghost was displeased at this and opened its mouth, showing rows of pointed teeth, while its eyes seemed to blaze with fire.

That was enough for Mrs Phillips. Facing up to a jack-in-the-box ghost was one thing but arguing with an apparition with pointy-teeth was entirely different. 'You should have seen us run upstairs,' Mrs Phillips later said.

There was never any rational explanation for that ghost, which seems to have decided to return to wherever ghosts exist, for there seem to be no record of any further appearances.

Strangely enough, a woman with the same name, Mrs Phillips, was involved in another ghostly incident. It might even have been the same person, acting as a ghost magnet in different locations in Wales. On this occasion, both Mrs Phillips and her husband, tenants in the house, reported strange occurrences in their home. It was the spring of 1899, two years after the Cardiff affair and happened in Burry Port in Carmarthenshire. This particular ghost liked to play the piano, so seemed to be reasonably amicable. It haunted the parlour, opened the piano, played and vanished whenever Mr and Mrs Phillips appeared.

Other things also happened, with objects moving around the house and people awakened at night-time. The owner of the house said he had not seen anything and when the house was thoroughly cleaned for the spring, the ghost took the hint and vanished with the dirt. However, it may not have travelled far as very shortly afterwards workers at the Copper Works tip reported unusual happenings. As often with 'real' ghosts as opposed to people wearing white sheets, there was no logical explanation. The next story is better known.

Abducted by a ghost

Llwynypia is one of a string of communities in the Rhondda Fawr Valley in South Wales. In 1893 it was heavily industrialised, with rows of houses running parallel to the river and along the valley sides. One of these streets was Amelia Terrace, a row of 20 houses. Number eight contained four rooms, with a pantry near the back door. In this house lived Mr Dunn (or Downe) from Somerset and Mrs Dunn. And into this house came a ghost.

As ghosts go, the Amelia Terrace ghost was not all that terrifying. It wore moleskin trousers and had what appeared to be a white sheet across its shoulders, which sounds more like a hoax than a spirit. On the credit side, it emerged from nowhere and vanished at will.

According to the tale, the ghost entered the house, lifted Mrs Dunn and carried her away. Here is the story in Mrs Dunn's words:

'I am the woman who was carried away, and I am the woman who can tell you the truth about it. I have plenty of witnesses who have heard the noise, and I had plenty of company in the house when he (the ghost) took me away. They asked the constable who looks after the company's houses to stop here a night to hear and see if he could, but he did not come. I was sitting on a chair by the fire with three other persons, - Mrs Lewis, Mrs George, and John Samuel. The company was outside.

It was at half-past eight in the evening as near as I can say when the ghost pulled me off the chair towards him to the passage. I was afraid, and I screamed and jumped back to my chair. He was still there. Mrs Lewis told me to speak to him. I felt too nervous at first, but after a time I started to speak to him, when, before I could finish my words he pushed me out from the house and across the bailey and into the water closet. Here he lifted me onto the seat, standing, and he pointed to the top of the wall. He told me in Welsh to raise the stone and take what was under it, and that I must go with him. That was all he said to me there.

Then he took me down about 200 yards from the house. I cannot tell you how he took me from the closet because I lost all control. I found myself by the brim of a pond. Here he took from me what I had in my hand and threw it into the water. Then he told me he should never trouble me anymore. So that's all the truth. I am not able to do the washing nor anything else; I am not the same woman that I was before, and I don't think I ever will be. I can give you these names and many others who can swear to what I have said: John Samuel, 9 Amelia Terrace; Mrs Lewis 1 Amelia Terrace, and Mrs George 11 Amelia Terrace.'

So that was that. Personally, I find it one of the strangest ghost stories I have ever encountered. There seems no reason for it. Was the intruder a ghost? If so it was a very solid spirit to lift and carry a full-grown woman. If it was a man, why ask Mrs Dunn to do something he was evidently able to do himself? If it was all a fabrication, what was the point? These questions remained unanswered and probably always will.

There was one theory banded about the village. The visitor had indeed been a ghost, the spirit of an elderly local man who had died in an asylum. He had returned to look for a bag of gold he had hidden, and once it was found, realised it was no use to him so threw it away. When the story circulated, many of the local people also began to search for the gold.

Pirates, smugglers, monks and now ghosts all seem to have one thing in common: they lose their treasure. How strange.

Haunted Farm

This story is short, sweet and simple. Aberdaron sits near the tip of the Llyn Peninsula in North West Wales. It is a small village, surrounded by farms. One of these farms is Bodwrdda, which in 1889 held livestock including a bull and sixteen cows. One summer morning, just as dawn greyed the eastern sky, the cowherd rose from his bed and stumbled toward the cow shed to milk the cows.

He had entered the farmyard before he realised that the cattle were all loose and milling about. Still tired, he began to round them up when the bull lowered its head and charged at him; ripping his shirt and slicing open his cheek with its horn. Bleeding and shaken, the cowherd returned to the farm and reported the incident to the farmer. Naturally annoyed, the farmer and the cowherd chased the animals back to the cowshed and called the police.

'We have a prowler,' the farmer reported.

The police took the matter seriously, and six tall policemen arrived to patrol the farm. They marched around, tapping their truncheons on the palm of their hands, but rather than find a flesh and blood vandal, they were witnesses to something uncanny. Three of the cow-house doors suddenly opened, and then closed simultaneously without anybody being present. The same thing happened again, and the police ran out, suspecting a prankster with a piece of string attached to the door handles. There was nobody there and no explanation. Not only that, but for the next few nights there were strange sounds. And then it all ended, as quickly and mysteriously as it had begun. Answers on a postcard please...

Haunted Mountain

In the 19th century, ghosts seemed to pop up all over Wales. Graveyards were the favoured locations, but they were also in streets and houses, canal towpaths and mines. There was even a ghost reported on a mountain.

In the 1870s the colliers at Blaennant Pit at Aberdare were a tough crowd. They worked long hours at a dangerous job and did not fear man, God or the Devil. Yet they were a little nervous about walking over Merthyr Mountain. There was a ghost on that hill, or so the rumour said. It appeared around midnight, perfect time for ghosting, and resided on a rocky ledge overlooking the miners' cottages at Blaennant.

While the men were either working in the pit or sleeping in bed at that hour, the women were nervous about the unknown ghostly thing that lurked on the ledge. The women ensured they were safe by locking their doors and windows, in case the ghost materialised into something more substantial than spectral. In the November of 1877 three miners missed their train to Merthyr and began to walk over the mountain together. The night, of course, was dark and cloudy, with occasional spells of heavy rain and the three men hurried, hoping to stop for refreshments at the inn of Pleasant View at the top of the hill. Apart from the hiss of the rain and the scream of wind, the only sounds were the crunch of their heavy boots on the ground and the occasional mutter of conversation.

As the miners approached Blaennant, the sky was darker than ever, but the nearby works provided occasional flashes of light from which they got their bearings. At the fearful ledge, the clouds parted, the moon came out, and the ghost was revealed. The lower half was black, it had its arms outstretched its head was white, and it made a shrieking sound as it waved its arms back and forward. The three tough miners turned and ran with the thing following them. The youngest fell and knocked himself out, to waken by the fireside in one of the Blaennant cottages.

'How did I get here?'

'We carried you,' his companions said.

That in itself was an act of courage. Naturally, the miners reported the incident and the police, used to ghost hoaxes, turned up in force. They scoured the hillside, helped by locals burning to end their women's worries. They found nothing. There was no trace of the black-and-white ghost and no clue as to its origin. The mystery was never solved, and the spirit never returned.

The Guardian Ghost of Vaynor

Vaynor is a village a few miles from Merthyr Tydfil in the Brecon Beacons National Park. In the 1890s, during a period of industrial unrest, the local miners walked out of work to gain safer working conditions. Being idle, the striking men were blamed for any misdemeanour in the neighbourhood, so when somebody damaged the boundary wall of Vaynor Churchyard, people glared at the miners.

When a miner from Cwmrhydybedd casually lifted a stone from the wall, either to repair or destroy, a ghost suddenly appeared. Once again the spirit was dressed all in white and once again it could assume corporeal form. It seems that Welsh ghosts had that useful little trick. The white-clad ghost assumed a deep voice and asked the miner why he was disturbing the abode of the dead.

Strangely, the miner did not give an adequate reply, which seemed to anger the ghost. Evidently powered with unearthly spirit-strength, the ghost grabbed the miner and dragged him to the nearby river. As it held him over one of the deepest pools, the ghost threatened to shove him in and hold him down until he promised to stay away from the graveyard.

Vandalism seemed to stop after that. I do wonder at these strange Welsh ghosts.

The Friendly Society Ghost

Sometimes, one never knew what a Welsh ghost would do. Some were just plain scary, while others looked after the people they left behind. This tale concerns one of the latter. By the late 19th century Friendly Societies were common across Britain. These societies were for the mutual benefit of the members, who each contributed a small sum each week, so when somebody was ill or in need, they would be paid from the society funds. In 1875 a government act regulated the companies, requesting effective auditing and a registration system. By the 1880s over 27,000 Friendly Societies existed throughout the British Isles, saving the members the horror of destitution and the Workhouse.

Wales was no exception to the rule, and the societies flourished all across the country, including Pontardawe in the Swansea Valley. One particular organisation had a strict rule that although they paid funeral expenses if any of their members died, they would not pay in the event of a suicide.

In the 19th century, suicides were frighteningly familiar. It is hard to lift and leaf through any contemporary newspaper without reading of at least one suicide. They were as common as Welsh ghosts. It was unfortunate then that when a member of the Pontardawe Friendly

Society died in unusual circumstances, the officials of the society suspected suicide.

When the society's officials refused to pay the deceased funeral costs, they soon began to experience his anger from beyond the grave. The first the officials knew of the man's fury was on the Sunday following the funeral, when the deceased's ghost appeared before one of the officials. It must have been an exciting encounter as the dead man demanded the money he was due in life. Not surprisingly the official refused, at which point the spirit attacked him, tearing the clothes from his back and chasing him down the road where the official took refuge in a public house.

The aggrieved spirit was not finished, and on Tuesday he made his presence known at the Society meeting at the lodge room, by giving the obligatory five raps on the door. When the members opened the door, nobody was there, yet a voice sounded: 'pay my widow my funeral money, and then I shall be at rest.'

The room emptied very quickly as the members scurried away. There seems to be no postscript to this little story, so it is hoped that the essential humanity of the society members overcame the strict adherence to the rules.

The Unexplained Ghost of Dowlais

Dowlais is an industrial village near Merthyr Tydfil, so not perhaps the sort of place one would expect to come across a ghost. However, spirits seem to come and go wherever and whenever they like and can haunt a coal mine as easily as any gothic mansion. In this case, the cemetery at Pant, a few minutes to the north of Dowlais was the scene of the haunting.

It was during the short summer nights of May 1890 that the sounds were first heard. They started about eleven, after dark, and kept local people awake for a while as they tried to work out what was happening. Some thought it sounded like a 'brood of goslings' and others like a child in distress or a young dog. People thought the sounds began near the cemetery gates, very loud at first and then gradually dying away. For a while there was no alarm over the noises until one elderly lady claimed to know precisely what it was, for she had heard the like before when she lived in Breconshire. She told everybody that it was a cry that preceded a death. Her words increased the discomfort of the people of Pant, and then things only got worse. A man was walking past the cemetery one night, and as he approached the gates, all was quiet and still. He saw something moving and what he described as a 'pack of dogs' passed right through the iron bars of the gate without a sound.

For a few weeks, people lived in apprehension, and then the sounds in the graveyard ended. There were no unexpected deaths and no more sightings of phantom dogs.

That was the thing about Welsh ghosts. Unlike Hollywood films, they seldom have a clear-cut ending. They come, they haunt, and they vanish without explanation and often without reason. Ghosts are strange things when all is said and done.

Chapter Fourteen
Is The Holy Grail in Wales?

King Arthur is one of the most famous literary figures in the world. There have been numerous books and films that feature the semi-mythical king, with a whole host of legends, stories and theories. He may have operated in Scotland or in Wales; he may have fought against the encroaching Saxons; he may have done this or done that. His sidekick Lancelot is as well known, as is his erring wife, Guinevere. An enduring legend surrounds the Knights of the Round Table and their search for the Holy Grail.

What was, or is the Holy Grail? Well, even that is disputed. Some say that the Grail was the cup that Christ used at the Last Supper before His betrayal, while others believe it was the container in which His blood was collected after the crucifixion. One version of the story claims that Joseph of Arimathea brought the grail to Glastonbury in England and founded an abbey there, in the first century, either immediately before the Roman invasion or shortly after. I wonder what the local Celtic Druids thought about that. The legends continued; the Knights Templar somehow got hold of the Grail, and in 1398 Sinclair – or St Clair – of Roslin in Scotland carried it over to what is now Nova Scotia. Alternatively, the Grail was stored in the Chalice Well in Glastonbury.

Naturally, with such a piecemeal history, many artefacts may lay claim to being the Grail, and one such sits securely in Wales.

Not only is it in Wales, but it is on public display and can be observed by anybody who chooses: how strange is that? It is a massive plus for Wales to have possibly one of the greatest treasures in the world with easy access for the public. This fantastic object is on display in the National Library of Wales in Aberystwyth.

Unfortunately, not much of that particular Welsh Grail remains; the object is also known as the Nanteos Cup, and according to the experts, it is the remnants of a mediaeval mazer bowl. The Nanteos Cup was held in the 12th century Cistercian Strata Florida Abbey at Pontrhyd-fendigaid in Ceredigion for an unknown length of time. When King Henry VIII of Wales and England decided to change the religion of his realm so he could swap wives, he dissolved the monasteries. It was probably the greatest religious and possibly the most significant social revolution in Wales for centuries and transformed the country. One of the abbeys thus terminated was Strata Florida.

According to the legend, which may well be reasonably accurate, when Strata Florida Abbey was dissolved, seven of the monks grabbed the Grail and ran. Not sure where to go in a time of great peril for Roman Catholic monks, they hammered at the door of Nanteos House, near Aberystwyth, and requested sanctuary. The family took them in and there they remained. When the monks eventually died, the Grail stayed at Nanteos.

Another version of the legend has an English origin, claiming that it was the prior of Glastonbury who fled to Nanteos, bringing an entourage of monks with him. While the prior became the family chaplain, the monks found work around the estate. Only when the last monk was on his deathbed did he tell the landowners, the Powells, that they had taken the Grail with them.

Of course, the Nanteos Cup might not be the Grail. Other legends suggest that it is a fragment of the True Cross on which Christ was crucified, or merely a communion cup from the abbey. What is not doubted is a strange power that the cup, or Grail, seems to possess.

For well over a century, the Nanteos Cup has been used to heal the sick. If anybody believed that using the Cup, or the Grail, would help them, they put down a deposit of whatever value they could afford and borrowed the artefact for a time and drank from it. Apparently, it was extremely successful, and many people were cured. However, there was a downside, for some patients actually gnawed the wood, presumably with the hope that imbibing the fabric would increase the efficiency of the medicine. Naturally, with sufferers chewing at the cure, the Grail began to shrink in size.

The house at Nanteos also changed. It was rebuilt in 1739 as a splendid Palladian mansion, for Thomas Powell, the Cardigan MP. Another of the same family, the eccentric George Powell whose friends included the poet Algernon Charles Swinburne, began to show off the Nanteos Cup.

In 1878 the Cambrian Archaeological Society displayed the Grail at St David's College, Lampeter in Ceredigion. Now it was out in the open, its fame spread and continued to spread, particularly in the opening decade of the 20th century when there was renewed interest in European mythology. It was possibly then that the association with the Holy Grail began. In 1967 the cup left Wales when the owners sold Nanteos and moved just over the border to Ross on Wye in England, taking the Grail with them. Then, in 2014, disaster struck when somebody stole the Grail. It was missing for a year and then recovered again in 2015. Now the Nanteos Cup or the Holy Grail is safe in the National Library of Wales.

Is this the Grail? Apparently not, the Nanteos Cup is made of wych elm, while legend says the Grail was of olive wood. Despite that minor blip, it is tempting to hope, and tempting to believe that such a sacred object should reside in Wales, the home of so many Arthurian legends. Even if the cup is not the Grail, but a much later object, the powers it seems to have would guarantee that it should be treated with respect, if not veneration.

Nanteos House, however, has another claim to strangeness in the ghost of a man in a cloak. He was seen as lately as 1984 when he interrupted a film crew. He is not alone, for there is a ghostly rider and two women. Most of these spirits are harmless, but one of the women is said to appear before a death.

Do we believe? Should we believe?

Chapter Fifteen
The Pembrey Hatchet Men

The word 'wreckers' was once one to bring a chill to the spine of sea-faring men. These utterly evil people frequented dangerous coasts, luring ships to destruction by employing false lights to confuse the navigators. The wreckers would wait for the vessel to run aground on fanged rocks and then pounce, cutting the throat of any survivors and robbing the corpses as well as raiding the cargo for anything that could be used, salvaged and sold. The south-west coast of England was notorious for such savages, but there was also a group in South Wales.

Not far from Swansea is Pembrey in Carmarthenshire, where wreckers operated. They were known as the 'Gwyr-y-Bwelli Bach', 'People with Little Hatchets' or the 'Little Hatchet Men' and they were justly feared by the seamen who sailed this coast. The wreckers used the hatchets to break up the ships when they looted them. Even without the hatchet men, the beach of Cefn Sidan in Carmarthen Bay was dangerous. In the days before radar, sat-nav or radios, when ship masters were very much dependent on charts and the stars, vessels homeward bound from the West Indies, the East Indies or North America could mistake the lighthouse at Lundy for that at Ushant and stray onto the coast of Carmarthen. It is hard to imagine the carnage that a single storm could cause when at a time of poor land transport, most goods were carried by sea and the seas off Britain were heavy with ships.

The authorities tried their best to protect shipping with lighthouses, lifeboats and marker buoys, but false lights can reproduce lighthouses, the early lifeboats were relatively primitive, and buoys could be moved or removed. The wreckers could counter any move the authorities made, with the advantage of a total lack of scruples or conscience.

However, the authorities could take vengeance on the wreckers. One particularly notorious man, Will Manney, worked as a servant at Court Farm in Pembrey. He had the reputation of being a ship-wrecker and a footpad – the contemporary term for a mugger. Around the 1780s, Manney was the terror of the area, haunting the Pembrey district and the Kidwelly road. When an elderly woman was found murdered the peacekeepers suspected Manney but could prove nothing. The only clue they had was a piece of ripped cloth in the dead woman's hand. The local magistrate, John Rees of Cilymaenllwyd, ordered a search of Manney's house at Pwll and when nothing was found, told his men to dig up the garden. Perhaps he was working with the word of an informer, for the diggers found Manney's coat, ripped and stained with blood. When Manney came to trial in 1788, a local tailor identified the coat as Manney's. The jury found the Manney guilty and he was hanged and gibbeted on Pembrey Mountain, which meant after the execution his body was left to be picked clean by birds.

Manney did not go with dignity and remorse. He swore and shouted at the crowd as the cart jolted him to the scaffold, fought the executioner, pushed away the chaplain and died kicking and struggling. Before the noose tightened around his neck, Manney cursed the magistrate John Reese and his entire family. The curse worked. Reese's grandson, John Hughes Rees, lost three of his daughters. Two drowned and one fell to her death; neither left any children. Wales can produce its quota of strange, wild men.

Despite this terrible example, the wrecking continued. One particularly famous wreck on this coast was that of *La Jeune Emma*, en-route to France from Martinique in November 1829. Among the passengers were young Adeline Coquelin, the 12-year-old niece of Napoleon Bonaparte, and her father, Lieutenant Colonel Coquelin. Lured on shore by signal fires, *La Jeune Emma* perished. Those of her crew who survived the initial impact created a makeshift raft of anything that could float. Some of the crew clambered on board, only for the frothing sea to capsize the raft. Most of the crew drowned, with only four men reaching the shore. Witnessing the fate of the raft, the remaining survivors clambered up to the rigging as the sea lashed the ship and the hull began to break up.

Dawn brought some relief as the decent people of the coast came to help. They rescued another two of the crew even as the wreckers began the systematic plunder of *La Jeune Emma*. The wreckers salvaged sherry and coffee, rum and ginger, spices and cotton and all they could use from the swiftly disintegrating ship. The authorities sent for the militia, but by the time they arrived, there was nothing much left to guard except three hundred gallons of rum. The hatchet men must have kicked themselves for missing such a lucrative haul.

The captain, together with the lieutenant colonel, young Alice and four crewmen were buried in St Illtud's graveyard in Pembrey. The sea claimed the other casualties but returned a few more bodies, tossing them ashore not far away, to be buried at Laugharne. Only six men survived out of the crew of nineteen.

When one of the graves at Laugharne was later opened, somebody had plundered the coffin of its body; grave robbers were still very much a plague in the late 1820s. The robbers had left the seaman's blue shirt behind, possibly because in those strange times, the penalty for stealing clothes was much more severe than the punishment for stealing a dead human body.

In December 1833, the local magistrate wrote a report to the Home Office about the looting of vessels at Cefn Sidan. The 370-ton barque *Brothers*, bound from Bahia to Liverpool had been wrecked on Cefn Sidan sands earlier that month, with 15 of the 16 men on board perishing. The magistrate commented that: 'What particularly induces me to address your Lordship, is, the nearly total plunder of the Wrecked Vessel and her cargo by the Country People'

There was no suggestion then that the local people had lured the vessel ashore but the magistrate reported that: 'as I followed the Seashore, I observed numbers of Country People employed in cutting open Bales of Cotton which were lying in quantities along the shore of nine miles in length and carrying them away in Bags and Carts etc... The People ... engaged in breaking up the wrecked vessel with Saws, Hammers etc. and conveying the timber etc. away in Carts.'

The local constable was too outnumbered to prevent the looting, and the looters attacked the magistrate when he tried to arrest them. That was the third wreck within a week. The magistrate continued: 'these disgraceful scenes will again occur, as wreckers are frequently on this coast and as I was myself this time Assaulted, there is no knowing to what lengths opposition may be carried, as they come prepared with short hatchets, hammers etc.'

The nearest harbour is now Burry Port, with the original harbour called Pembrey Old Harbour. However, the area has more than hatchet men and grave robbers. In the 19th century gunpowder was manufactured here, and in the Second World War, the RAF had an airfield, with the usual tragic legacy of crashed aircraft. Naturally, such a history has produced a plethora of ghosts. Some say that the hatchet men still lurk in the woods, waiting for a full-rigged ship to grind ashore. Others have seen the spectral image of ships sailing toward the beach, crewed by men long dead. There are also a few people who have seen an airman from the Second World War, complete with flying helmet as he still defends the country from the horror that was Nazism. Every corner and every village in Wales seems to attract its ghosts. It is indeed a haunted country.

Chapter Sixteen
The Coast of Mystery and Myth

Although the popular image of Wales jumps from the mountains of Snowdonia to the south coast cities and the pits and ranked houses of the valleys, there is much more to the country. As well as the magnificent castles there is the 870 miles of coastline, imbued with history, legend and story. Many of the stories are as strange as one will find anywhere in the British Isles.

It is not the intention of this small book to cover every mile; that would take a much larger volume. I only intend to pick out some of the strange and interesting parts. The question is not what to put in, but what to leave out. For a start, what can I say about the area around Bosherston? Again, I will write this chapter with small pieces separated by subheadings.

Huntsman's Leap

Bosherston is a strange place perched on one of the wild headlands of Pembrokeshire. As well as possessing a lake with three prongs, it is the closest settlement to St Govan's Head. Now, many people in

Britain will identify Govan with Glasgow in Scotland, but this Govan is pure Wales and totally fascinating.

Wales is crammed with places named after saints, and some of these holy people deserve their sanctity for the lives they lived and the inaccessibility of the homes they chose. Saint Govan is no exception. One day he was out for a contemplative wander when a boatload of roving pirates hove into view. Back in St Govan's 6th century, these pirates would probably be slave raiders from Ireland, the same sort of gentlemen who grabbed St Patrick. Well, Govan had no desire to be a slave in Ireland, so he fled. As he was in God's favour, the rocks opened up, and closed around him, hiding him from the predators. When the pirates departed, the rocks opened again, and Govan decided to stay in the area and convert the heathen. Such strange events seem to have been common in old Wales.

However, the pirates were not finished with Govan yet. They returned and sneakily pinched the silver bell from Govan's chapel. Once again the forces of good intervened and angels recovered the bell and increased its volume a hundredfold so Govan's message could reach even more people.

Saint Govan's tiny chapel, twelve feet by twenty feet, is halfway down the coastal cliff-face, with a flight of steps that are not for the faint-hearted, particularly on a windy day. This particular chapel is not the original. Indeed it is pretty modern, dating from around the 13th century; seven hundred years or so after Govan departed Wales for a more ethereal type of heaven. There is another legend that claims one of St Govan's bells is embedded within the rock, but if you rap your knuckles on the cliff-face, the bell will ring. Other legends suggest that there are different numbers of steps when going down to the chapel rather than going up from it, and the name Govan is from Sir Gawain, a Knight of the Round Table, who retired here when King Arthur died. Wales has a plethora of these interwoven legends.

Mention of St Govan's bell brings to mind the bell of St David's Cathedral at Whitesand Bay. The story is similar, except that rather than thieving pirates, the devil heard the melodious church bells calling people to Christ, so he sent down a squad of demons to grab them. The demons sauntered around, looking very much like men. They heard the church bells, snatched them carried them out to sea and dropped them, laughing demonically. However, the power of good can overcome the force of evil and the bells still ring. Before a storm, they sound to warn mariners of coming foul weather – according to the legend. We have space for a last bell-ringing legend before moving off to other things. The estuary at Ferryside has a lost village beneath the water. If you doubt that, go to the water's edge on a quiet Sunday morning and listen for the sound of the church bell. We will meet another lost villages later.

Not too far away from Govan's chapel is the 120-foot deep geo named Huntsman's Leap, which is a favoured spot for cliff-climbers. This geo itself is amazingly impressive, a chasm that reaches down from the top of the cliff to the often-boiling sea. The strange story of the huntsman is worth the telling.

According to the story, a group of men was chasing a lone horseman, possibly even a huntsman. I never did find out who he was or why he was being chased, but he reached the geo, put spurs to his horse and leapt across. He touched down on the far side, took a deep breath and looked back and down, and down, and down. The sight of the chasm and the turbulent sea below was too much for him, and he died of fright.

If pirates, saints and daredevil horsemen are not enough, then have a look out to sea. If you are fortunate, you may emulate a farmer named Harry Reynolds. In 1782 he was walking alone near Linney Head when he saw a merman. Harry dashed home to tell his friends but when he returned the merman was gone, and so too, possibly, was his credibility as an accurate observer.

The mermaid's curse

There was another mermaid sighting at Stumble Head. According to the story, many years ago a farmer was striding along the beach when he came across a mermaid sleeping just below the high tide mark. Now, mermaids, as everyone knows, are unchancy creatures with strange powers and the farmer thought that he could capture her and use her powers to make himself immensely wealthy. Even better, if he could get her pregnant, their children would be gifted in ways he could not imagine. The temptation was overwhelming, and he stepped cautiously toward the sleeping creature and enveloped her in his arms.

The poor mermaid screamed in horror at having this great hairy human grabbing at her, but it was too late. Lifting her, the farmer carried the terrified little creature to Treseissyllt Farm, ignoring her cries for help and her tears that were as salt as her sea. Once in the farmhouse, the farmer thrust the distraught mermaid into a small room with no view of the sea and no possibility of escape. To make doubly sure, he tied the mermaid tightly down and smiled upon his prey.

'You belong to me now,' the farmer said. 'And you'll make me rich.'

So what would a poor mermaid do in such circumstances? Well, a Welsh mermaid would sing. All night long, the mermaid sang, with her voice invoking the slow hush of the waves and the mystery of the long horizons and hidden currents of her home. In the pre-dawn dark, as the farmer tried to block the melancholic music from his head, he heard somebody outside his house. He listened to the hiss of whispers and the muted slide of something on the grass, and once the rap of knuckles, or possibly flippers - against his window.

'Who's there?' The farmer sat up in bed, wishing he had the foresight to leave a weapon in his bedroom.

The only answer was a sudden gale that rattled all the windows and crashed open all the doors of his house. Rising fearfully, the farmer ran to the mermaid's prison. She was gone, with the ropes with which he had tied her lying snapped and useless on the floor. The farmer ran outside and to the beach, only to see the shadowy shapes of mermaids sliding back into the sea.

Before she plunged into the sea for the last time, the mermaid turned around. Knowing that the farmer had sought children, she called out 'no child shall be born in your house for generations to come.'

Her curse worked, and it was centuries before a baby was born in Treseissyllt. However, all is forgiven now, and the farm now has a camping site and much more friendly owners.

Although mermaids are not as common off the Welsh coast as they have been elsewhere, there are other mermaid stories. Off the cliffs near Aberystwyth in 1826 a dozen people ogled as a mermaid was seen washing herself as her tail flicked around her. Not sure why a mermaid had to wash as she lived under water, but perhaps she was a strange mermaid.

One last mermaid story comes from Conway. Conway Bay is the home of the lost palace of Llys Helig. The palace owners were extremely unpleasant people, so God quite rightly sunk the palace in the sea. In the past, people believed that they could see the palace ruins when the tide was low, but unfortunately, this is not true as the visible rocks are natural. However, the story of the mermaid may be true. One poor mermaid came ashore and lay on the rocks pleading for help. As nobody helped her back into the water, she cursed the town of Conway. It's best not to mess with a Welsh mermaid!

Lost land in Cardigan Bay

If you look at a map of Wales, the country appears to be a huge mouth, with the open jaws on the west. The gaping mouth is Cardigan Bay, facing onto Ireland as if daring raiders and pirates to come across the sea and be eaten by the Welsh dragon. That may be an inventive concept, but no more strange than the legend of the lost land in Cardigan Bay.

Many centuries ago there was a fertile land within the confines of Cardigan Bay. It was known as *Cantre's Gwaelod* – the name may mean the 'hundred of the lower region'. This land was a fertile plain until the sixth century AD when the sea rushed in and drowned the land and all it contained. This submerged territory was said to extend from Bardsey Island in the north to the town of Cardigan in the south. It contained sixteen 'fair cities' or settlements and must have been low-lying as a series of embankments and sluice gates held back the sea. The story said that a man named Seithenym, the steward of Gwyddno Garanhir (Gwyddno the long-legged), was in charge of the sluice gates. When one day Seithenym got drunk and did not close the sluice gates in time so the sea broke through. That was the end of Cantre's Gwaelod.

Mrs Aelwen Prichard gave me a slightly different version of the story. She took me to the coastline and pointed out various land-and-seamarks as she did so. According to Mrs Prichard, the gatekeeper was Seitheuyn rather than Seithenym, and he was the prince of the land. Mrs Prichard insisted that the sixteen cities were the grandest in Wales except for Caerlon-on-Usk and after the near-Biblical flooding, Seitheuyn's six sons including a youth named Tudno all entered the college at Bangor. Tudno later became the patron saint of Llandudno.

Unravelling myth from folklore is nigh impossible in Wales, and that is part of the strange charm of this country. According to the website of St Tudno's Church in Llandudno, the young Tudno entered the monastery of *Bangor is y Coed* in the 6th century and later carried Christ's message to Llandudno, so Mrs Prichard knew her stuff. The website also confirmed that Tudno was a son of Seitheuyn (I kept Mrs Prichard's spelling) and adds that the gatekeeper was the son of Seithyn Seidi, King of Dyfed.

Just as I was getting comfortable with that legend, Mrs Prichard added another version. She had a wicked smile on her face as she told me that there was a possibility that Seitheuyn was actually not the sluice-keeper but another of Wales's ubiquitous princes. He was in Cantre's Gwaelod to woo a delectable lady named Mererid, who was the keeper of the sluice gates. Seitheuyn and Mererid were so intent on their personal pleasures that they failed to notice the storm and left the gates open, thus causing the flooding. To me, if not Mrs Prichard, that sounds like a variation of the Garden of Eden story. Indeed the whole story could be Biblical, with the drowning of the land a very vague memory of the time of the Great Flood. Now that is strange.

The last Ice Age was at least 7,000 years ago and possibly another 10,000 years before that. However when the ice caps melted, causing devastating floods, it must have been life-altering for the people of the time. Given the undoubted trauma, stories would have been created and repeated from generation to generation, each one altering as life gradually changed.

The earliest existing written record of the Cantre's Gwaelod legend is in the 1250 Black Book of Carmarthen, which includes the poem *Boddi Maes Gwyddno*, which translates as *The Drowning of the Land of Gwyddno*. That poem corresponds with Mrs Prichard's second version of the legend.

According to legend, when the sea is flat calm and the weather quiet, it is possible to see buildings under the sea. That combination of good weather and calm conditions does not often happen on the west coast of Wales, so my advice is to grab any opportunity that occurs as the next window might be a long time in coming.

I am going to deviate here for a few lines, to give a few examples of other strange ideas of Celtic royalty. If the stories are true, one Welsh king had his own foot scratcher. This unfortunate individual had the job of holding the royal feet all evening and scratching them. Equally to be pitied was the Yeoman of the Cowdung, while the king's porter had the enviable luxury of keeping all the entrails of animals slaughtered in the royal kitchen. He could also scoff any toasted cheese the king happened to leave behind. In return, he had to find clean straw for the king's bed. No luxurious feather mattresses in those days.

And so back to vanished lands.

There is another, much later ballad about the bells of Aberdovey that sometimes can be heard ringing in Cardigan Bay when the waves shake the bells in the tower of a long-abandoned church. The English language version of the ballad first appeared as late as 1785, but it might be a translation of a more traditional song. The first verse of one version runs:

If to me as true thou art
As I am true to thee, sweetheart
We'll hear one, two, three, four, five, six
From the bells of Aberdovey.
Hear one, two, three, four, five, six
Hear one, two, three, four, five and six
From the bells of Aberdovey.

A number of causeways run seaward into Cardigan Bay. The longest is known as Sarn Badrig and extends for some 13 miles off Harlech in Merioneth. It is also known as St Patrick's Causeway. Others are Sarn-y-Bwch off Towyn and Sarn Cynfelyn which extends seven miles, just north of Aberystwyth. Could early humans have built these causeways? After all, early humans built the amazing circle of Callanish in Lewis and to create Stonehenge they had to transport massive blocks of stone from Pembrokeshire to far off Wiltshire. These maritime causeways may have given rise to the legend of the lost land, but geologists insist that they are not man-made but are natural submarine ridges of rock created by an accumulation of pebbles and boulders derived from glacial deposits although it is possible that man has added to them at some time.

In 1770 William Owen Pughe, an antiquarian who created an English-Welsh dictionary claimed that he took a boat beyond Sarn Cynfelyn and saw an ancient fortress called Caer Wyddno, the fort of Gwyddno.

'*I sailed over the ruins on a very calm day and thus for about three minutes I had a clear view of them, and many of the stones seemed to be large slabs and lying to confusion on the heap.*'

This place is the legendary home of the king of the sunken land but, alas for romance, the perceived ruins are also purely natural, being only a jumble of stones and boulders placed by the tide.

However, scientists agree that at one time Cardigan Bay was dry land, with forests and probably people, at least 7,000 years ago. It is possible that folk tales have retained a memory of this land. I wonder if the stories of Lyonesse and Arcadia also come, distorted and vague, from memories of these very ancient lands. People tend to wear rose-tinted glasses when remembering the 'good old days', so perhaps the sunken land was viewed as an earthly paradise, an Atlantis full of wisdom and apple trees. Or perhaps that's precisely what it was. In Wales, the strange is normal. After all, where else would somebody build a statue to a ghost?

Statue of a ghost

It could only happen in Wales. Statues are created to commemorate famous people or important events. Kings and queens, generals and writers, philosophers and sportspeople all have statues built to their memory, but only in Wales could there be a statue of a ghost.

Talacre Lighthouse at Point of Ayr was first built in 1776, a time when the United States was beginning its life as an independent nation. It is on the coast of Flintshire, guarding the sea routes to the major port of Liverpool and in 2010 a new resident took temporary residence. Seven feet tall and made of stainless steel, the figure stood on the balcony, reflecting the light from the sun and gazing down on the beach below. The owner of the no-longer-working lighthouse, James Mc Allister had the sculpture placed specifically to commemorate the ghost, with whom it shared the balcony. Local artist Angela Smith was the sculptor, using chicken wire to create the frame and adding shaped cardboard, which a blacksmith named Richard Jones replaced with steel. So much for strangeness, but what about the ghost? So many people claim to have seen it that there must be some truth behind the legend, although nobody seems to know who the man was.

According to local lore and a whole host of witnesses, the real ghost stands on the balcony in full uniform and with a sailor's cap placed neatly on his head, as if he is proud of the job he does. And so he should be.

The area has seen a great deal of maritime trade through the centuries, from the Roman garrison at Chester to the packet rats who worked the vessels from Boston to Liverpool in the 19th century and the Atlantic convoys in the 20th. When the Industrial Revolution swept across Britain in the 18th century, trade increased, and the lighthouse rose at the Point of Ayr, Wales' Furthest North, to protect ships sailing into the estuary of the River Dee.

Like many of the early lighthouses, the weather proved too powerful for the engineering of the time, and in 1819 the lighthouse collapsed. The present 58-foot- tall structure replaced it, with a light that was visible for nineteen miles. The names of the keepers are known through census records, such as Samuel Brooks and his family in 1841. Perhaps one of these men is the resident ghost.

When the lighthouse was replaced by a new version, the ghost stories began. People reported seeing a man in an old-fashioned frock coat busily cleaning the lantern, which would be a daily task for the keepers. The authorities took note, suspected somebody had intruded into their property and checked the building, to find nobody there. In fact, the door was locked, bolted and padlocked so nobody could have entered the lighthouse to clean the lantern. Sightings continued, enhanced by reports from sundry walkers who reported that they felt sick even passing the building while dogs and other animals refused to pass at all.

When the building was re-occupied as a lookout position during Hitler's War, nobody seems to have seen the ghostly keeper but immediately it was abandoned in 1945, the ghost returned. Presumably, he did not like to see his old home empty. Once again, people saw the man in the frock coat and once again people began to feel sick when they passed the lighthouse. One man, Jeffrey Moses, tried to buy the place in 1966, but caught some illness and sadly died. The sightings continued and attracted such attention that in April 2006 a full squad of ghost hunters arrived with all the most up-to-date paraphernalia. Naturally, they found all sorts of things, with strange sounds and when they held a séance, a spirit that claimed to be a lighthouse keeper named Raymond said he had died of some unspecified fever. Another medium claimed a spirit named Daniel or Samuel contacted her.

Today the lighthouse still stands, but the sculpture has been removed, so no friendly seven-foot-tall metal giant watches over the people who throng the beach. Is the lighthouse haunted?

If so, it is not alone. The South Stack Lighthouse near to Holyhead off Anglesey is also haunted, apparently by the spirit of a man with the splendid name of John Jack Jones. This 1809 lighthouse has an impressive position with nearly 400 downward steps from the main island leading to a fragile-looking suspension bridge across a dangerous chasm that winter gales can lash to utter white-fanged fury. It is open to visitors, but it is far better to come on a calm day, as John Jack Jones discovered the hard way.

In October 1859 he was crossing the iron bridge to the lighthouse during a storm, and a rock fell on him. Severely injured, he tried to get inside the lighthouse but the howl of the gale cancelled his calls, and he remained outside all night. He died three weeks later. Strangely, his father, John Jones, died at the same lighthouse in 1828. Today John Jack Jones can be heard rapping at the windows and doors as he tries to enter the building.

South Stack had an unfortunate reputation for early keepers. The first two keepers, James Deans and Hugh Griffiths, could not rub along, and in such a confined space, friction can be dangerous. Griffiths eventually replaced Deans as the head keeper, and later got rid of his new assistant. After that John Jones arrived and remained for 18 years. When he died in 1828 his widow, Ann Jones took over. Now that is also strange, having a female lighthouse keeper in 19th century Wales. But why not? She had lived in the lighthouse for 15 years and knew the workings inside out.

Final Words

A few final words before we leave the coast. It would be impossible to say farewell to the Welsh coast without mentioning the sea serpent that appears and disappears off Barmouth in Merioneth. The first recorded monster-mention was in 1805 when the creature attacked a vessel in the Menai Strait. The monster was said to have coiled itself around the ship's masts, and the crew eventually forced it overboard. However, the serpent was persistent and followed the ship for a couple of days. Such sightings were relatively frequent in the 19th century when ships were smaller, slower and quieter as well as closer to the water.

In saying that, this sea creature or its descendants seemed to prefer to hug the north Welsh coast, surfacing off Llandudno in 1882 and again in 1937. In 1971 strange footprints appeared near Llanaber and four years later a gaggle of girls witnessed a creature with 'a long neck and a square face and a long tail'. There is no explanation.

Now for a brief mention of a couple of ghostly ships. Off Porthcawl in Glamorgan are the Sker Rocks. The vessel *Le Vainqueur* struck these rocks and sunk. Her master was cast ashore dead. The ship is sometimes seen heading for the shore, while the master appears as a corpse candle. Most ghostly vessels seem to have appeared in the distant past, yet as recently as the late 1960s, people saw a ship off Abergele. According to legend, this was the ship of Madoc, which appears and disappears. The warriors inside were said to be quite clear.

I have one last thing to add. Wales is a land of strange superstitions and one centres on the Cereg of Gwyn rocks at Penrhos. In this place of often-wild weather, people used to see strange lights hovering a few days or a few hours before a vessel was wrecked. These lights were known as corpse lights and showed before a death. True or not, the idea is strange enough to close this chapter on the Welsh coast.

Chapter Seventeen
Warriors of Wales

I mentioned a Welsh redcoat in an earlier chapter, for the figure of the British redcoat was once feared by her enemies across the globe. But why did British soldiers wear red coats? Possibly because 12th-century Welsh soldiers wore red coats.

Wales is renowned for her fighting men. Welsh warriors kept Roman legions at bay, defended the country against invading Anglo-Saxons and often fought the Normans to a standstill. During the Anglo-Scottish wars, thousands of Welshmen fought on the English side and proved to be amongst the toughest opponents the Scots faced. Welsh archers arguably won the Battle of Falkirk against the Scottish freedom fighter William Wallace, and Welsh infantry and archers fought formidably for various kings of Wales and England against France. When a small Scottish and Royalist army lost the Battle of Worcester against vastly larger Cromwellian forces, there is a strange tradition that a small group of Scottish Highlanders escaped as far as Dorstone, where the place name Scotland Hill commemorates them. A company of Welshmen, fighting for Cromwell, surrounded the Scots but rather than face them in open battle, sent in their dogs, which ripped the fugitives to pieces. If that proves anything, it demonstrates that Welshmen fought with their heads as well as their spears and arrows.

What made the Welsh such fierce warriors? Gerald of Wales, who toured the country in 1188 to raise men for the Third Crusade, thought he knew. Gerald said *'The English are striving for power, the Welsh for freedom; the English are fighting for material gain, the Welsh to avoid a disaster.'*

Gerald also wrote that *'The Welsh people are light and agile... Not only the leaders but the entire nation are trained in war. Sound the trumpet for battle, and the peasant will rush from his plough to pick up his weapons.'*

With such a background, it is not surprising that Welshmen should make such excellent warriors. The history of Wales and England are inextricably intertwined. With English and Welsh wars, Norman and Plantagenet encroachment, a Welsh king of England and a shared border, it could hardly be otherwise. However, this chapter is not about Welsh fighters *per se*, but the strange side of Welsh soldiers. Our first look is at a Welsh warrior who is often neglected, yet who turned the tide of Welsh and English history.

History tells us that Rhys ap Thomas came from Llandeilo in Carmarthenshire. He was the man who solved England's dynastic problems one day in 1485 when, at the Battle of Bosworth Field, he lifted his poleaxe and chopped down King Richard III. There is nothing strange about that; killing is a soldier's trade. However, before he disposed of the English king, Rhys had a slight problem to overcome. At a previous time, Rhys had sworn an oath that Henry would only take the crown 'over his bellie', and in those days when one's vows meant something, Rhys could not break his word and fight against Richard.

Accordingly, Rhys travelled to the bishop of St David's and asked him to remove the oath. The bishop was also a man of honour and said he was unable to lift a sworn oath. The bishop told Rhys that he had to take the traditional route and allow Henry to step over his prone body. At first Rhys believed that was an impossible ask, but eventually, he thought of a way. When Henry led his army across Mullock Bridge in Pembrokeshire, Rhys lay face up in the river underneath, thus fulfilling his oath and allowing himself to join Henry's army.

Once Rhys had disposed of Richard, the Tudor leader, Henry, and Rhys remained friends, with Rhys rewarded with lands in South Wales. Other Welsh soldiers had their own strange tales.

William Nott

There is a statue to General Sir William Nott in Nott Square in Carmarthen. Unlike many Victorian officers, Nott was not from a privileged background but was the son of an innkeeper, rising to a general in the Indian Army and fighting through the First Afghan War. However, this little piece of writing is only using General Nott to gain access to his father, who ran the Ivy Bush Inn in Carmarthen. Nott's words to his clients deserve to be remembered: 'come in, eat, drink, be merry and pay Nott.' Welsh soldiers are strangely smart, although there are occasions when they dress a little too formally for war.

Who would wear a top hat to a battle?

A Welshman would, of course. Lieutenant-General Sir Thomas Picton's name is well known to any student of Napoleonic warfare. He was the Welshman who led a division of British infantry at Waterloo. However, he had a picturesque career before that. Born in Poyston in Pembrokeshire in 1758, he joined the army aged 15 and in 1794 was based in the West Indies. As governor of Trinidad, he became known for his harshness, and there were strong rumours of torture and worse. Despite his record, in 1806 a court found him not guilty of 34 counts of cruelty and guilty of one, for which a retrial found him not guilty as the island was at that time under Spanish law, which permitted torture.

Picton fought through the Peninsular War, gaining a reputation for profanity, scruffiness and ferocious discipline. On the credit side, he led from the front at the battles of Busaco, Fuentes de Onoro, Ciudad Rodrigo, Vittoria and Badajoz. Knighted for his services, Picton was shot in the hip at Quatre Bras but bandaged the wound himself and kept his injury quiet so he could fight again two days later at Waterloo. Some accounts say he led his men into battle while dressed in a black frock coat and a top hat, others say he wore a nightshirt and a top hat. His final few minutes were controversial; some accounts say that a French cannonball blew off his hat, while others say that one of his own men, sick of his cruelty, put a musket ball in his head.

Either way, his dying words were recorded as: 'come on you rogues, you rascals' to his men. When Wellington objected to the crude, foul-mouthed man being interred in St Pauls, Picton's body was buried in a family vault in Hanover Square, London. Later in the century, he was re-interred in St Paul's in London, ironically close to the Duke of Wellington. Picton is the only Welshman to be buried in St Paul's Cathedral and possibly the only general to charge into battle wearing a top hat.

Singing Soldiers

Generals and lords get plenty of publicity. Most military books, fiction and non-fiction, deal with the exploits of the great, if not necessarily the good. The ordinary Welsh soldier, the rank and file, the hard living, hard swearing men who wore the uniform, took the risks and casualties and who did the actual fighting, are barely mentioned. So here is a mention of one strange fact, taken from the *Western Mail* of 24th March 1915 when the First World War was in full swing.

In that day's *Western Mail*, the Methodist missionary Mr E. Stanley Jones was lauded for giving a lecture on 'War and Music' to the Newport Literary Society. 'Wherever these Welsh are, they will always be found singing, they will fight to the last ditch with a song on their lips, and they will die, if needs be, as they have lived, with a song on their lips.'

His words were backed by an unnamed Army surgeon, who said that the only songs he heard in the firing line that were 'not of the music hall type' were sung by a 'famous Welsh regiment, the men of which were the only soldiers, as far as he knew, who sang in parts.'

There were other occasions when Welsh soldiers demonstrated their musical talent. The 11th Welsh Regiment gave a concert at Hastings Town Hall in December 1914 with violins, cellos, solo singers and piano performances. The next year, in October 1915 the 114th Welsh Brigade was renowned for its singing with the 13th Welsh Regiment outstanding.

No doubt there were many other occasions, but these few are sufficient to show the strange Welsh habit of singing even through what was possibly the most horrific war in history. Those of us who have reached a certain age will no doubt remember the film *Zulu* when the 24th Foot and the Zulu warriors had a singing match. Unfortunately, that incident did not happen. In that battle of Rorke's Drift, the majority of defenders were not even Welsh. The Welsh reality, in the continual horror of the First World War, was even more impressive, moving and a bit strange.

The Welsh Arab

Probably most people in the Western world have heard of Lawrence of Arabia, either through historical knowledge or because of the 1962 epic film. Fewer people will be aware that Lawrence was Welsh-born, with Scottish and Irish parents and a strange life and career. Thomas Edward Lawrence was born in August 1888 in Tremadog, Gwynedd, the illegitimate son of Thomas Chapman from Westmeath and Sarah Junner, half-Welsh and half-Scottish.

Educated at Oxford, in 1910 Lawrence became an archaeologist for the British Museum, working in the northern Sinai and probably also laying the groundwork for future British military operations. Joining the Army in an intelligence role, Lawrence remained in the Middle East where in 1916 he liaised with the Arabs in the Arab Revolt that made him famous. With the war won, Lawrence worked in the Foreign Office, but his hope for an independent Arab state was dashed when Britain and France carved up much of the Middle East between them. Perhaps the disappointment helped Lawrence's decision to renounce the limelight for he joined the RAF as an ordinary airman. He died in 1935 in a road accident, a tragic end for one of the First World War's most iconic and undoubtedly strange, warriors.

Female Warrior

If you are ever fortunate enough to visit Kidwelly Castle in Carmarthenshire, look out for Gwenllian. She won't be able to say much because not only is she a ghost, she is also headless. Gwenllian was a female warrior who fought the Normans. Her full name was Gwenllian ferch Gruffydd, and she lived from around 1100 until the Anglo-Normans killed her in 1136. Married to Gruffydd ap Rhys, the prince of Deheubarth, Gwenllian was heavily involved in an uprising against the Anglo-Norman invaders. Gwenllian was captured near Kidwelly Castle, and the Anglo-Normans beheaded her.

So what is strange about this warrior woman? Apart from the fact that she was the only known Welshwoman to lead a Welsh army, there is a spring bearing her name. It came into being at the place the Normans executed her. The strangest aspect is that she is not better known. Her ghost remained in Kidwelly Castle, but according to legend, her haunting stopped when somebody found the head and buried it next to the body, although not that long ago somebody reported seeing her again.

There is no doubt that Welsh warriors and Welsh soldiers were amongst the bravest and most skilled anywhere. Were they strange? You decide.

Chapter Eighteen
Strange and Haunted Castles

Wales has many castles, probably more per square mile than any of the other nations of Great Britain. Such a plethora of fortifications shows the turbulent nature of the inhabitants who were determined to resist any invader. Such a plethora of fortifications also gives many atmospheric buildings for denizens of the spirit world to frequent, or for strange tales to collect. This chapter will look at only a few of the reputed 600 castles that grace, or once graced, the landscape of Wales.

Carreg Cennen

One of the most interesting of Welsh castles is Carreg Cennen at Trapp, near Llandeilo in Carmarthenshire. The site of the castle is incredibly old, with human remains found that date back thousands of years. Historians and archaeologists believe there may have been an Iron Age hillfort here for centuries before the mediaeval castle was built. The Romans may also have been here; certainly, their coins have been found on the site, although Roman wealth may have been spoil from a raid or tribute paid to the local ruler.

Urien Rheged, Lord of Iskennen, is said to be one of the earliest owners of one of the Carreg Cennens while his son Owen, surprise, surprise, was said to be one of King Arthur's knights. The Arthurian connection would place these gentlemen in around the 5th or 6th century AD, hundreds of years before the present castle existed.

It was around the 1190s that Lord Rhys, Prince of Deheubarth and son of Gwenllian ferch Gruffydd built the first 'proper' castle here and ensured that it remained in Welsh hands. In 1248 the unpleasant Norman intruder Matilda de Braose was ready to hand the castle and power to the Norman English but luckily her son, Rhys Fychan grabbed it back. After a see-saw of control over the next half-century Edward Plantagenet of England laid his rapacious hands on Carreg Cennen, and after that, the English were in control.

Carreg Cennen's castle's position is impressive, with far-reaching views, but many of Wales' castles can boast the same. However, in the whole of Wales, only Carreg Cennen can boast a vaulted passageway and an underground cave. According to legend, during a siege one of the castle garrison was sent to bring water from a spring in a nearby cliff. As the man was at the spring, the besiegers found him and killed him. Learning from the soldier's death the masters of Carreg Cennen created the passage so the castle would never run out of water.

With this being Wales, there were stories that the castle's water supply had its own magic and a legend that Owain and fifty picked men are waiting in the caves beneath the castle. When Wales needs them most, they will awaken and sally out, either to save the nation or to bring peace to the whole world. Owain must have been some warrior in his time. There is an additional legend that the water is also a wishing well, and if you leave a pin or pins, the wish may come true. It is possible that the water was sacred long before the castle was built, with the legends relating to Druidical sacred practices. In Wales, *anything* is possible.

Haunted Caerphilly Castle

The second largest castle in Britain, Caerphilly cannot fail to impress. Its very size proves that the builder, the Anglo-Norman Gilbert de Clare, had immense respect for his adversary, the Welsh Prince

Llewellyn ap Gruffudd. At 30 acres in extent, Caerphilly was built to dominate Glamorgan in South Wales and was the first in Wales and Britain to have a concentric ring of walls. Often attacked, it has a story of battle and siege. One strange sight is the Leaning Tower of Caerphilly, a legacy of a siege by Oliver Cromwell's men. The Roundhead's cannon damaged one of the towers in 1648, which has been tilting like a drunken man ever since.

Naturally, such a place has its ghost and its stories. One enduring legend tells of the spirit of Princess Alice de la Marche of Angouleme, the niece of Henry II. Alice was a fascinating woman, sophisticated, loving and, of course, beautiful. Unfortunately, Alice was married to Gilbert de Clare who seemed to prefer warfare and fighting to keeping his wife company.

Tired of being neglected by her brutal husband, Alice became interested in the Welsh Prince Gruffudd of Brithdir, sometimes, and perhaps tellingly, called Gruffudd the Fair. The two became lovers, but Alice was a devout Christian and confessed her sin – if that is what it was – to a monk. The monk was less than trustworthy, broke his oath of confidentiality and told Gilbert de Clare. The Anglo-Norman lord was incensed at being cuckolded and sent Alice back to France. With his wife out of the way, de Clare ordered his men to scour the area for Gruffudd.

In the meantime, the Welsh prince had learned about the monk who betrayed his sweetheart. Hunting the treacherous confessor down, Gruffudd took the monk to the nearest tree and hanged him there and then. The spot is still known as Ystrad Mynach, the Monk's Vale.

However, de Clare's men were equally adept at hunting and hanging. After scouring the area, they located the unfortunate Gruffudd and hanged him as well. Intent on rubbing in his success, de Clare sent a rider to France to tell Alice of the death of her lover, no doubt adding gloating details. The second she heard the news, Alice collapsed and died. Although Alice never returned to Caerphilly her ghost did. When the moon is full, Lady Alice walks. Dressed in green, she haunts the ramparts of the castle. Some say that she wears green to mark her husband's jealousy, but perhaps there is a deeper reason. Green is the Celtic holy and magical colour and the green lady could be a guardian spirit from long before the time of Lady Alice, a symbol that, despite the success of Anglo-Norman arms, the old Celtic spirit of Wales still exists, waiting for a resurgence in fortunes to reclaim the land.

Denbigh Castle

Denbigh Castle in Clwyd was one of Edward Plantagenet's 'ring of castles' that were built to encircle the tiny and utterly defiant Principality of North Wales. The castles were England's final act after centuries of English and Anglo-Norman aggression had conquered Wales. Now an impressive ruin, Denbigh is home to a whole clutch of ghosts, most of which seem to gather on the Goblin Tower and the triple-towered gatehouse.

The Goblin Tower has a horrible dark *something* moving around, which could be why the boy who stares from one of the windows appears so disconsolate. The boy may be the son of the Norman castle builder who is said to have fallen from the tower. People who seek more drama claim the youth was caught having a love affair with Lord Henry de Lacy's daughter and de Lacy ordered him thrown from the tower. There is also the ghost of a woman who carelessly dropped her baby down the well. She is heard crying, apparently, and probably has cause for legend says the baby was the son of the castle's owner, Henry de Lacy and he would not be pleased to lose his son and heir.

As this is Wales, it is almost obligatory to have a dragon. A man with sixteen fingers killed this particular dragon – and there must be a lot of that story hidden. I'd love to hear the Welsh original. Finally, there is a white lady who visitors can meet in various places around the castle grounds, although her favourite haunt is around the Goblin Tower, where a white mist surrounds her. There is so much in one ruined castle that a visit is necessary to feel the spirits in this building. I have one more castle about which to write: Ogmore.

The Ogmore treasure

If anybody was so inclined and very fortunate, he or she could spend a lifetime travelling around Wales digging up all the buried treasure. The wealth at Ogmore Castle, a few miles from Bridgend in Glamorgan, may prove a little tricky, however. *Y Ladi Wen,* the White Lady guards this one and woe betide anybody who tries to find it. The Lady's vengeance will fall on him or her, as it did on whoever tried to say where it was hidden.

There is a story behind the legend, but I can find no information regarding the identity of the White Lady. Ordinarily, local lore is all too keen to provide names and details for such stories. In this case, there is a tale that an un-named man woke to find the White Lady beside him. The Lady took him to Ogmore Castle and showed him where to find a pot of gold, ordering to only take half. Now incredibly rich, the man left the castle, only to return later for the remainder of the gold, despite the Lady's instructions. Inevitably, the White Lady caught him and took away his good fortune. He died a pauper but never revealed the location of the treasure. And that incomplete little story ends this chapter on strange castles.

Chapter Nineteen
Animal Lore

In common with most Celtic peoples, the Welsh have an affinity with animals. They are known for their skill at raising sheep and have many legends where animals are prominent. For instance, in the old days of kings and princes, the kings had their own cat, which was valued at fourpence, the same as a goat. The cat had to have good eyes, ears, teeth claws and tail; had to be a good mouser and not eat her kittens. If anyone killed a cat, he was fined as much wheat as would cover the cat when she was hung up by the tail with her head touching an even floor. That was a lot of grain and shows the value even a king placed on his moggie.

Naturally, the ferocious Welsh warriors also kept animals, although mainly horses and dogs, Even today, Welsh infantry regiments have animals on the strength, none more so than the Royal Welch Fusiliers.

The Royal Welch Goat

Now the First Battalion, Royal Welsh, The Royal Welch Fusiliers have a history as illustrious as any regiment in the British Army, and that is to say as distinguished as any in the world. They fought at the Boyne and Blenheim, faced Bonny Charlie's Jacobite Highlanders at Culloden, advanced at Minden, defeated the rebels at Guildford Court

House and refused to surrender the Colours when surrounded by superior numbers at Yorktown. They suffered the Egyptian heat in 1801, slogged through the Peninsular campaign against Bonaparte, showed immense gallantry fighting the Russians at the Alma, sweated and bled in the Indian Mutiny, marched across the African veldt between 1899 and 1901 and earned undying fame in France, Gallipoli and the Middle East in 1914-18. From Dunkirk to the horror of Kohima, the Royal Welch continued their battling in the Second World War and later in Bosnia.

That was a rapid potted history of the 23rd Regiment of Foot. The 41st (The Welch) Regiment is equally as impressive, but one record will have to do. This book is not a military history. As for the old spelling *Welch*, the Royal Welsh (with an s) regiment was known until (or part of it was) as the Royal Welch (with a c) Fusiliers. The spelling is archaic, and the regiment seemed determined to retain it for the sake of tradition.

It is not known when the Welsh regiments began the tradition of marching with a goat. The goat is part of the regiment, rather than a mascot. It is understood that the goat was already established as a member of the 23rd Foot in 1777, during the American Revolutionary War, while in 1844 Queen Victoria gave the title 'Royal' to the goat along with an animal from her own royal herd. When Victoria started the royal herd, the goats were in Windsor; now the royal herd is in Whipsnade Animal Park, and from here the regiment chooses its goats. If no suitable goat can be found in Whipsnade, men hunt one down from the wild herds of North Wales, where they seem to prefer the headland of the Great Orme to anywhere else.

In 1855 a goat also arrived on the muster roll of the 41st Regiment as they fought through the Crimean War. Naturally, there are legends behind the regimental goat. The following little anecdote seems to come from that war and may relate to the 41st Foot. A young Welsh soldier was on picket duty one bitterly cold night, and a kid goat wandered close. The sentry either felt sorry for the young goat, or more likely intended to eat it, but he grabbed the creature and thrust it under his great coat. Exhausted by the stresses of the siege of Sebastopol, the sentry subsequently fell asleep. When a Russian patrol approached, the goat began to bleat loudly. The bleating jerked the sentry awake; he saw the Russians and fired, alerting the rest of his company who stood to and chased away the Russian patrol. From that point, according to one version of the legend, the goat was taken onto the regimental strength. I did ask Mrs Prichard her opinion, to be told that she had never been in the Welsh Army and knew nothing about goats.

There is another, lesser-known goat tale from the Crimea. At some point in the siege of Sevastopol, the 23rd were stationed near to the French Foreign Legion. The Legionnaires were hardy soldiers with a reputation for toughness and looting. A group of them wandered over to the Fusiliers, befriended the goat and fed its keeper cognac. The next night they returned and poisoned the goat.

Shocked at the sudden death of one of their own, that same afternoon the Fusiliers buried the goat with full military honours. During the night the Legionnaires acted as body snatchers and recovered the goat. Perhaps they ate the flesh, but one man undoubtedly skinned and cured the fleece, making a lovely warm winter coat as protection against the bitter wind. As soon as spring approached, the Legionnaire decided that he no longer required his beautiful goatskin coat and sold it to a British officer, reputedly a captain of the Royal Welch.

Meanwhile, back in the headquarters of the Fusiliers, there was a bit of a puzzle. The regiment had a tradition that the goat should parade in the Officer's Mess on St David's Day. Without a goat, that tradition would have to be shelved. However, the Fusiliers would not be denied, and on the 1st of March, true to custom, a shaggy goat walked into the Mess, until the time came for the Loyal Toast. As soon as the Queen's name was mentioned, the goat stood to attention and Private Styles, resplendent in a sheepskin coat and with a goat's head attached to his cap, drank his glass of champagne and returned to duty. I hope the Fusiliers still continue the strange old tradition of having the smallest of the regimental drummers ride the goat into the Officers' Mess on St David's Day.

There was another loss during the Mons retreat of 1914 when the 23rd's goat died. Even though the entire German army, infantry, cavalry, artillery and possibly Kaiser Bill himself, was advancing at speed just beyond the horizon, the Fusiliers halted to pay respects to their goat. While artillery shells whizzed overhead and burst in the neighbouring fields, the Fusiliers buried their goat with full military honours in a small Belgian graveyard. Those Belgian civilians who had not already fled watched with disbelief, thinking that the Welsh were strange people indeed.

By tradition, the goat of the 1st battalion Royal Welsh is named Billy, with the second battalion's goat Taffy and the 3rd battalion's goat named Shenkin. In saying that, there seems to also be an official 'proper' name for the goats, for Taffy of the Welch Regiment also being known as Gwilym Jenkins. Naturally, the goats have their own uniform, with the goats of the second and third battalion sporting a natty green coat with gold piping, enhanced by the regimental crest, while the poor old goat of the first battalion has to go naked except for his fur. Some armies may reckon that regimental goats are strange; in Wales they are essential.

Despite the importance of goats in Wales, only in that country is there a village named after a dog.

Death of a faithful hound

The village of Beddgelert in Snowdonia must be one of the few, if not the only, community in the country to be named after a dog.

The gist of the story is something like this. When the old princes of Wales were not engaged in fighting, they enjoyed the hunt, so kept a pack of hounds. Llywelyn ap Lorwerth, otherwise known as Llywelyn the Great, was no exception. He lived in the 12th century, a time of turbulence when the Anglo-Normans were attempting to invade and conquer the country. Llywelyn's favourite dog was Gelert, who was fierce as a dragon during the hunts but gentle as a new-born lamb at other times. Indeed, Gelert was so mild that Llywelyn allowed him free reign inside the house, while all the other dogs were confined to the kennels. Llywelyn trusted Gelert so much that one day he took his lady wife hunting, leaving the hound to guard their baby son.

The hunt was a success, and Llywelyn returned home happy and hungry. Gelert greeted the hunters at the door of the hunting lodge, but something was wrong. The hound was covered in blood. Llywelyn ran into the lodge, desperate to check on his son. The cradle was upside down, with a spreading puddle of blood underneath and the covers tangled, ripped and bloody.

Shouting in his anger and grief, Llywelyn drew his sword and hacked Gelert to death.

Only then did he hear a small sound from the cradle. He set it to rights and saw his son, still alive under the blood-sodden covers. Beside the baby lay a massive wolf with its throat torn out and blood on its fangs. It did not take Llywelyn long to piece together what had happened. The wolf had attacked the baby, Gelert had killed the wolf in a savage fight, and now he had murdered his faithful hound. Llywelyn was beside himself with sorrow for his favourite dog, and buried him nearby, with two stones to mark the grave. The nearby village, Beddgelert, is said to mean 'the grave of Gelert' in honour of the dead dog.

It is a poignant story of love, loyalty and betrayal, and like many such stories, it may not be entirely accurate. In fact, it is a complete fabrication. In the late 18th century 'romantic' tourism was becoming popular, boosted by poets such as Wordsworth and Sir Walter Scott. The English Lake District was popular, as was Scotland's Trossachs, both famed for their wild scenery of mountains and water. A gentleman by the name of David Pritchard, who ran the Goat Inn in Beddgelert hoped to improve the tourist trade in Beddgelert, so apparently, he created the legend. He had no need to alter the name of the village for it was already the Grave of Gelert. However, rather than a dog, Gelert, or possibly Kelert, was supposedly a Dark Age monk from the area.

Whatever the truth of the story, it worked. People came to Beddgelert to look at poor Gelert's grave and still, do. There is a plaque to tell the story, yet it is strange that such falsehood was required, for the village is beautiful enough not to need such a false attraction.

Of course, King Arthur has to get into any Welsh strange story topic, and dogs are no exception. Arthur's favourite hunting dog was named Cavall, and he came to fame while hunting Twrch Tryth, a tremendous supernatural boar. Cavall was such a powerful dog that when hunting Twrch Tryth, he left a deep imprint of his foot on a rock. Arthur saw the print and raising a cairn, placed the marked rock on top. People began to come to see this cairn they named Carn Cabal, and somebody stole the marked stone. That was pretty pointless, for however much they coveted the Cavall's footprint, the rock had a mind of its own and always returned to the spot from where it was taken.

My final strange story features fish rather than animals and concerns an event that took place at Aberdare on Wednesday, 9th February 1841. It sometimes rains in Wales; it has to, or the rivers and lakes would dry up, and the hills and fields would lose their greenness. However, on that February day, the rain did not consist of water but of small fish, with the largest only five inches long. John Lewis, a sawyer, said that they fell down the back of his neck and filled the brim of his hat. The fish came in two separate showers and covered an area about 80 yards by 12 yards. The day was 'uncommon wet' and somewhat breezy but not with a wind sufficiently powerful to blow shoals of fish from the sea.

In May 1932 a similar phenomenon occurred at Graaf Reinet in South Africa when a dozen fish fell from the sky. High flying birds were blamed, which could not be the case at Aberdare. In Chihuahua in Mexico in 1925, a storm rained fish that supposedly had been sucked up from the sea by a waterspout. Perhaps something similar happened in Wales?

We only know that it was strange.

Chapter Twenty
King Arthur in Wales

I grew up in Edinburgh, Scotland's grey old capital, in the shadow of the extinct volcano of Arthur's Seat. As a boy, I heard the legend that King Arthur and his knights were sleeping under the hill, waiting for the call to come and save the country. The legend of King Arthur is known all over the English speaking world. There are places named after Arthur all over Britain, from central Scotland to south-west England, yet possibly there are more in Wales than anywhere else.

Welsh Arthurian sites range from Bosherston Pools in Pembroke, which is supposed to be where Arthur received his sword Excalibur to one of many possible locations for his grave at Coetan Arthur, a circular barrow at St David's. There is even an indentation in a rock a few miles from Aberdovey called Carn March Arthur made by the hooves of Arthur's horse.

A quick look for the lake where Arthur received Excalibur revealed eight possibilities (doubtless there are more). The Bosherston candidate is now also known as the Lily Ponds, which is situated not far from Pembroke. Other Welsh claims include Llyn Llydaw, about ten miles from Llyn Ogwen in Snowdonia, which is another possibility, and Berth Pool near Baschurch. Outside Wales, there are sites in Cornwall and in Dumfriesshire in Southern Scotland, both areas where the indigenous inhabitants would be of British stock, the same as Arthur could have been. There is also one site near Glastonbury.

Other Welsh sites named after Arthur include Arthur's Stone at Cefn Bryn in West Glamorgan. The legend says that Arthur found the giant rock in his shoe, removed it and threw it away. Archaeologists, however, always willing to spoil a good myth with irritating facts, claim that it's more likely to be a Neolithic burial site.

There are many more sites, too many to give each its own story, so I will only list some of them, with a small point of interest. For example, West Glamorgan has Cefyn Bryn, also known as Arthur's Stone or Arthur's Quoit. When the moon is full, a man in glowing armour is said to emerge from the stone. Would that be Arthur himself? At Celliwig in Coedkernew, there is a Neolithic burial chamber. This ancient place was said to be the site of King Arthur's Court even although it belongs to a time thousands of years earlier.

Underneath Chepstow Castle, there is a cavern in which sleeps King Arthur and his knights. The legend says that on one occasion a man saw them and fled when he nearly woke them up. A suspiciously similar story centres on Llyn Llydaw, where a shepherd came across a hidden cave in which King Arthur and his knights sleep. Unfortunately, the shepherd tripped and hit a bell, the sleepers awoke, and the shepherd fled. Arthur is also said to be waiting within the caves at Craig-y-Ddinas at Pont Nedd Fechan in Mid Glamorgan. Perhaps the spirit Arthur can flit from place to place, and why not? He was active in life so why not in death? It would be strange if an energetic man became a passive ghost.

There is another Arthurian connection at Llyn Barfog at Tywyn where a monster used to rampage around until Arthur drowned it. However other sources claim it was not Arthur but a warrior named Huw Gadarn. That may be true, for Arthur was also busy in Snowdon, where he banished a giant, who is buried on the summit.

That is enough of the small pieces of Arthurian lore. I am sure you get the idea that Wales is full of Arthurian connections and that begs the question: was King Arthur Welsh? Which leads to another question: was Arthur, even a king? In Arthurian tales, mythology, history and fable weave in and out in an intricate Celtic knot that even the Dark Age experts have difficulty trying to unravel. So I may as well have a shot and further muddy the waters.

The first mention of the historical Arthur appears in Aneurin's epic poem *Y Gododdin*, which seems to have been written in the early 7th century. *Y Gododdin* is a heroic poem about a Celtic war band that gathered in what is today Edinburgh in Scotland and rode south to fight the invading Saxons or Angles. Three hundred strong, the war band was defeated by much larger numbers at the battle of Cattraeth, which some historians believe may be Catterick in today's Yorkshire.

The poem lauds many of the warriors by name, including one man who was a good fighter 'although he was no Arthur.' That single line would suggest that in the very early 7th century Arthur was already a hero so famous that he needed no further introduction and even brave warriors paled in comparison. As *Y Gododdin* was written in what is now known as Welsh, we can guess that Arthur was of that same basic stock, that is, one of the Celtic, British people.

The question – or one of the many questions about Arthur – is to which part of the world did Arthur belong? Any glance at a historical atlas of the period will show that the British peoples were under assault. For the purpose of this little discussion, I am calling the Celtic peoples of the British Isles, from roughly the Firth of Forth in Scotland, south to Kent and south-west to Cornwall, 'British.' At that time, north of the Forth the people were known as Picts, and across the Irish Sea, the people were Irish or Gaels. Once the Romans withdrew, these neighbouring peoples viewed the now-defenceless British as easy prey. From the north, the Picts raided and attacked. From the West, the Irish raided for slaves and loot and sometimes settled, and from the European mainland, the Germanic tribes of Angles and Saxons attacked, massacred and settled.

Assailed on all sides, the Celtic British fought back. It was probably at this time that Arthur appeared, or somebody that later chroniclers called Arthur. If we give him a time frame of around 540 to around 590

AD, we may be accurate, or as accurate as the combination of history and mythology allows. I am aware that thousands of people will have many arguments to dispute my claim and will happily bow to anybody who has firm evidence to prove their point.

Next is the problem of a specific place. With Arthurian legends spread so widely, from Angus in Scotland to south-west England, but all within or on the fringes of, the old Celtic-British area, we are reasonably safe to assume Arthur was British rather than Pictish or from one of the Germanic Anglo-Saxon tribes. Southern Scotland, South Western England, and Wales all lay claim to Arthurian sites, and it is possible that all are correct. Perhaps Arthur was commander of a war band of British warriors who roamed from place to place, fending off Germanic, Pictish or even Irish attacks wherever he was needed. Nonetheless, the Glastonbury claim, where in 1190 monks said they had discovered the bodies of Arthur and his queen Guinevere in Glastonbury Abbey, we can dismiss as spurious. It appears that the monks were attempting a confidence trick to attract pilgrims or money. It is also possible that King Henry of England, heavily engaged in a war against the Welsh princes, encouraged the 'discovery' to ensure that no Welshman claimed to be a reconstituted Arthur come to lead the Celtic Welsh against the Norman-English.

There are nearly as many Arthurian theories as there are Knights of the Round Table. One of the strangest suggests that Arthur was the brother-in-law of the mythical Lot, after whom Lothian in Scotland was named. Add to that the possible connection with Aurelius Ambrosius, who was a Roman official and may have been involved in repelling Saxon or Angle raids from the continent, and we have an incredible complexity of lore and myth. To clarify one point, Ambrosius was no king but may be remembered as a dominant military commander at a time of high stress – as might Arthur.

If Arthur can be identified as contemporary with Loth of Lothian, then how did the Arthurian tales travel to Wales through what became Anglian dominated land? Welsh tradition speaks of the *Gwry y Gogledd* – Men of the North – who moved down from what is now southern Scotland to drive out Irish settlers in Wales before settling there themselves. These men from the north may have been the descendants of the warriors who died at Cattraeth, moving south through the Cumbrian corridor, or even by sea, after the Anglian kingdom of Northumberland expanded into Lothian. If this movement occurred, then perhaps they carried with them more tales of Arthur, for they would have originated in the same area as *Y Gododdin*, with its mention of Arthur, was written.

There are so many theories and a dearth of evidence. Yet there is no doubt that Wales, or the Welsh people, fell in love with the Arthurian legends. Possibly, just possibly, King Arthur was a Welshman, fighting against the encroaching Anglo-Saxon tribes and the stories are all local. One prominent Welsh story concerns a battle at the City of the Legion.

When Nennius wrote his *Historia Brittonum* around 828 AD, he included a list of the battles of King Arthur, without identifying where they were situated. That frustrating omission has led to generations of historians gnashing their teeth and propounding wild theories. One battle that Nennius mentioned was at the 'City of the Legion.' Now, that statement could mean half a dozen sites in the southern half of Britain, where the Roman legions were based. One strong contender might be Caerleon in South Wales, now a suburb of Newport. There was a large Roman fort here to overawe the native tribes, and a relatively substantial civilian settlement clinging outside the walls.

We will never know how many people discussed the tales of Arthur in these early medieval days, but when Geoffrey of Monmouth put quill to parchment in the 1130s and wrote *Historia Regum Britaniae*, he added to Arthur's fame. Geoffrey kindly provided what he believed was the city of the legion's location: 'in Morgannwg, on the River Usk, not far from the Severn Sea'. That could only be Caerleon. However, much of Geoffrey's work is highly imaginative, as what passed for history was in those days, and still is in many cases. About half a century after Geoffrey's time the poet Chretien de Troyes mentions Camelot and the coincidence of names with Caerlon gave the world one location for Arthur's capital. If the Dark Age Arthur was in this Welsh town, he might have been in the castle mound or the Iron Age hill fort. Was Arthur here? If he were based in Wales, then Caerleon would have been a good place, with access to the sea and a surrounding spread of suitable agricultural land.

Indeed, some legends claim Arthur never left the city. He is said to be still there with his knights, waiting inside the Mynde until he is needed. People cannot wait to interrupt that poor man's last rest.

So there we have my take on it, culled from a hundred books and a dozen maps, with a bit of thought and some wandering prose. Was Arthur Welsh? By race, certainly (if one can call the British people a race), by location – well, Wales, as the most British nation of the British Isles, would be a natural place for Arthur to remain. Given a choice, would he not stay there? I rather think he would.

However, it would be rude to have a chapter on Arthur without including at least one mention of Merlin.

Not far outside Carmarthen on the Llandeilo road, the passenger may notice a strangely shaped hill on the left. This hill is Merlin's Hill, where, according to legend, that enigmatic fellow lived in a cave. Merlin is also said to be imprisoned in the hill by a spell cast by his witchy sweetheart. There is also the rock known as Merlin's chair, where he sat contemplating the view and casting prophesies. Nobody knows where Merlin's cave is, but the fortunate can still hear Merlin moving about inside the hill, clanking his chains in frustration.

Whether or not Merlin was ever here, his hill is the site of one of the largest Iron Age hill forts in the area and must have been a place of importance around the time of the Romans.

Merlin is also remembered by Carreg Myrddyn, Merlin's Stone, a standing stone near Carmarthen where Merlin was reputed to have hidden his treasure. Why did all these people in the past have treasure and what compelled them to hide it? That is indeed a strange thing. Anyway, there was a prophecy attached to this menhir that said a raven would drink a man's blood from the stone. Ravens and crows were often seen as birds of ill-omen in Celtic mythology, even before the time of the Norse. In this case, the story goes that one day a naïve man was digging for Merlin's treasure and it fell on him. A passing raven saw the corpse and fluttered down to feed, drinking his blood.

True or false? Either way, it makes a good story. Merlin would have approved. The legends, mystery and location of Arthur remain unproven, waiting for a historical breakthrough.

Chapter Twenty-One
Tree Lore

The Welsh, in common with other Celtic people, have an affinity with nature. Their folklore and strange legends include stories about animals. It also has myths about trees. As the previous chapter was about Arthur, it is only logical to begin this one with his trusted confederate and druid, Merlin.

Merlin's Oak
When Merlin's Oak shall tumble down,
Then shall fall Carmarthen Town

Many towns have trees growing in prominent places, but only Carmarthen in Wales had a tree that had to be protected to save the place from destruction. Merlin's Oak once stood on a corner site at Priory Street and Oak Lane, near enough smack in the centre of the town.

According to legend, King Arthur's famous magician Merlin was born in Carmarthen. Indeed the very name of the town is said to derive from Merlin, or Myrddin, as the correct spelling may be. When Merlin was a very young boy, he enjoyed playing in an oak tree, until he learned that some evilly-disposed person planned to chop it down. At that point, Merlin is said to have made the above prediction about the oak, although other versions claim that when the tree falls, there will be a significant flood. Is there any truth in this strange legend?

Probably not, as more sober, if less entertaining historians claim the tree was more likely planted to celebrate Charles II restoration as recently as 1660.

Either way, by the 18th century Merlin's Oak was a favoured spot for people to gather and gossip, which annoyed the less socially-inclined so that when the century turned, an irate spoilsport tried to poison the tree. Merlin's Oak never recovered, and the poor old thing finally died in 1858. Unhappy that their town might collapse, the good people of Carmarthen did their best to protect what was left of Merlin's Oak, with a stone base and spiked railings to keep off vandals or protect the public from various pieces of falling tree. However, the tree continued to deteriorate, and in 1951 one of the branches fell off. The Carmarthen people preserved it in the County Museum. In 1978 another vandal set fire to all that remained and the council removed the charred, battered stump. The remnants were moved to Saint Peter's Civic Hall in Nott Square.

And then the town held its breath, waiting for the inevitable destruction as Merlin's prophesy took effect. The people expected... And waited ... And nothing happened. Life continued as before. There were no earthquakes, volcanoes or raiding Vikings, only a little Welsh rain. Or rather, quite a lot of Welsh rain. It was like St Swithin's Day, and even Noah would have been apprehensive. The River Towi burst its banks and flooded the town, so proving the prophecy to be at least partly correct – or was it merely coincidence? There had been other floods in the past. However, people did murmur about tempting fate and the strangeness of it all.

Perhaps that is why somebody planted another tree to replace Merlin's Oak. Hopefully, it will protect the town against further flooding. Other Welsh trees are also justly famous.

The Bleeding Elm

Nevern in north Pembrokeshire has some interesting trees but none more so than a yew tree near to the 6th century St Brynach's church.

Brynach himself was sufficiently strange to warrant a second mention. He was a lady's man before he became a Christian, and the ladies returned his favours with interest, and apparently with passion as well. Whatever amorous techniques Brynach possessed, he used them well, and women sought out his company. Unfortunately, one such woman did not approve of Brynach suddenly taking the Cross and the vow of chastity and showed her disfavour by attacking him with a spear. Once he had survived the lady's attempt to perforate his now-holy-person, Brynach set about building a church. It was not an easy task, as the local demons did their best to torment him, and then when he had his wood all cut and ready to use, the local pagans stole it. It was enough to test the patience of a saint. However, Brynach persevered and eventually completed his church. Apparently, he also had a habit of walking to the nearby hillfort of Carn Ingli where he spoke to angels, which may have helped.

More serious historians give a less colourful version of this tale. These historians claim that Brynach was an Irishman who arrived in the area around 540 AD. He met St David in Pembrokeshire, which is presumably where Brynach converted to Christianity. Once Brynach was Christian, the local lord, Clether granted him land to build a church, and as Clether lived at Carn Ingli, the Godly may have misinterpreted Brynach's visits to Clether as trips to talk to angels by the Godly.

Even after the passage of some fourteen hundred years, fragments of the chapel survive, including what is known as the as the Vitalanus Stone with the words *Vitaliani Emereto* carved on it. The words meant nothing to me until I read they may refer to Vortimer, the son of Vortigern who we already met digging for dragons. Near to the church is the Great Cross of St Brynach which is an impressive piece of carving which boasted a strange tradition. On the feast day of St Brynach, 7th April, the local people met at the cross, waiting for the first cuckoo of the year.

I know that this chapter is supposed to be about trees, but strange Wales always diverts me onto other things.

The path in St Brynach's churchyard is lined by yew trees, one of which is known as the Bleeding Yew. This tree is reputed to be 700 years old and emits a blood-red sap from a scar six feet above ground level. Naturally, such a strange event has attracted stories. One claims that as Christ was crucified on a cross, the tree is bleeding in sympathy. Others say that a holy man, perhaps a monk was hanged from this tree for a crime he did not commit, and before the noose tightened, he said the tree would bleed forever to draw attention to his innocence. There are also those who say the tree will bleed until a Welsh price sits in nearly Nevern castle or until world peace breaks out.

Near to the yew is the thousand-year-old Braided Cross Stone, which is also an unsolved mystery. It is unique, with two cords braided to form the cross.

There are also rumours that Nevern Church is haunted by a man in a long white robe, while children are heard playing and laughing in the ancient building. The ghostly man wears clothes that were fashionable in the 6th century so he may be from the original Christian settlement. The nearby castle, naturally, also has a ghost, for terrible screams are heard from within the walls, and sometimes long drawn out sobbing. It was said that after the cries are heard, the temperature drops significantly. Some people have seen a man with a beard and an unusual hat, like the cup of a bra.

So much for the ghosts and bleeding trees, but the strangeness of this village does not end there. Near the ruined castle is the Pilgrim's route, an ancient path that slices into the side of the hill. If one looks carefully, one might see a Christian cross carved into the rock. Now even more strangeness begins, for some people say that the cross is marking a walled entrance to a secret cave. Such a place, in such a location, can only be interesting. The theories extend from King Arthur (again) secreting away the Holy Grail (again), to the equally strange story that the Knights Templar hid away the True Cross.

But these diversions take us away from the trees. There are other strange yews in Wales, such as the Pulpit Yew which is at Nantglyn in Denbighshire. This tree is so vast that church-goers mount a series of steps to a pulpit inside the trunk. There are strange old stories that claim that the yew was the original tree of life in the Bible, and cuttings were taken from Eve's yew and brought to Britain, where they still thrive.

As I discovered, in Wales anything is possible, and every strange event or legend leads to another, even with trees.

Chapter Twenty-Two
It's Customary in Wales

While some Welsh customs have their counterparts in the other nations of the British Isles, others are unique to the country. In this chapter, I shall endeavour to mention the purely Welsh, with apologies to those that I place incorrectly. Some are sensible to the time and place, some are strange, and some are pure and utterly weird. Once again I must thank Mrs Prichard for keeping me right on several occasions, with a poke in the ribs and a 'hey, that never happened.'

Courting custom

One custom that is charming is the idea that when young men visited their girls, they should carve a love spoon. There are many of these pieces in the Welsh Folk Museum in St Fagans, most very beautiful with hearts and Celtic designs. Perhaps the idea was to prove affection; although Mrs Prichard suggests it was more likely to keep the hopeful suitor's hands busy and away from his girl. As the father of two once-teenage daughters, I can understand that idea.

I must mention the strange practice of *Carny n y gively*. In the olden days, when people mostly lived in the countryside, courting could be an arduous ordeal. Roads were poor or non-existent, the weather was often inclement, and young men had to fit courting their future wife in between the demands of the land or other labour. It became reasonably normal to travel to the house of the young woman and stay the night. However, the parents of the intended bride had their own methods of ensuring nothing untoward happened, while allowing the young couple time alone.

The courting couple slept in the same bedroom – there would be no spare rooms in the house anyway – and even in the same bed. If that sounds fun, the girl's parents had other ideas. Both youngsters were placed in separate linen bags, and the girl's mother tied them in to ensure there was no hanky-panky. The bags reached up to the youngsters' necks and had no holes for the arms. Mrs Prichard told me that her grandmother actually sewed her mother into the bag. Perhaps that was common, or perhaps Mrs Prichard was merely proving a point.

The following morning the girl's mother would come in bright and early to release the couple from their confinement. When you think about it, *Carny n y gively* has many advantages. It allowed the couple time alone to talk yet without any unwanted complications and permitted the girl's family to view their prospective son-in-law. It would also be a lot warmer for the man than spending the night in a draughty barn.

Another courting custom occurred each 31st October, All Saints Day, which was the last day of the old Celtic year. In south Wales, it was common for a young woman or man to walk to a crossroad at midnight, shut their eyes and turn around three times. Simultaneously they shouted out the name of the man or woman they hoped to marry. If an image of that person appeared, then they would marry. If not, then they would have to find somebody else.

Even for the successful, things were not straightforward as it seemed customary in Wales to put as many obstacles as possible in the path of true love.

Wedding customs

Some of the Welsh wedding customs were normal, others verged on strangeness, and one or two must have been invented to put the word 'strange' in the dictionary. I could not find any time period for most of these, so I only presume they are no longer in vogue. Knowing Wales, I could be completely wrong.

Once the young woman and her man agreed to marry, they arranged a gathering of their friends. This was not a mutual hen-and-stag party but a formal meeting to decide how much the dowry should be. Presumably, there was a lot of haggling and tension on these occasions before the final agreement was written down. With the business side of things sorted, the couple would contact the *gwahoddwr*, the bidder, who officially invited guests. His system was simple, walking from house to house with a staff decorated with ribbons. Everybody would know who he was and would gather round. With this being Wales, the gwahoddwr often sang his invitation. One of the kindly librarians in the Welsh National Library found me this 1762 invitation:

'The intention of the bidder is this, with kindness and anxiety, with decency and liberality for Einion Owen and Llio Evans, he invites you to come with your goodwill on the plate, bring current money, a shilling or two, or three, or four, or five, with cheese and butter; we invite the husband, wife and children, menservants and maidservants from the greatest to the smallest. Come there early; you shall have victuals freely and drink cheap, stools to sit on, and fish if we can catch them, but if not, hold us excusable and they will not attend upon you when you call upon them in return. They set out from such a place to such a place.'

In parts of Wales, weddings traditionally took place on a Friday, with the newlyweds' house being furnished the previous evening. Again, there was a formal agreement as to who provided what in the new house. The bride was responsible for providing the bed and bedding, a chest, press and cooking utensils, while the groom found chairs, tables and everything else. Before the industrial revolution, virtually all of

Wales was rural, and the farmers' wives ensured the bride had the essential foodstuff to begin her new life.

The evening before the wedding, both parties met at the groom's house and the next morning, nursing hangovers, they separated again. Scores of the groom's friends collected their horses and reassembled at the groom's home. One chosen group rode to the bride's house and formally demanded that she come with them while the women inside the house locked and barred the door and refused them entry. In a tradition that could only happen in Wales, the bride's party and the groom's party engaged in a poetry and prose competition, each praising themselves and often castigating their rivals.

At length, the bride's party relented and allowed the groom's men to enter. There would be a bout of drinking, and then both parties continued the strange game. The groom's party closed around the bride to ensure she reached the church as the riders from the bride's party ambushed them at every crossroads to attempt to kidnap her. The groom's men were known as scouts as they defended the bride and it was not unknown for the bride and groom to tire of the game and gallop away together.

Despite all the play-acting, the wedding nearly always took place. However, the customs continued after the ceremony. It was once common to fasten the church gates and force the happy couple to pay to get away. On the journey from the church to their new home, people would stop the wedding party to wish them luck, and there was another, stranger tradition of stretching a rope across the road to prevent the carriage from passing. Once again, the groom had to hand over a monetary tip before the party could continue. On one occasion the groom was a Scotsman who did not know the tradition. He responded by thumping the first man who asked him for money and was starting on the others when the police arrived. He spent the day in a police cell rather than with his bride. That was not the best start to married life, but death also had its quota of strange customs.

Funeral Customs

Death was not something taken lightly in old Wales. After lying in the house for a while, the corpse was carried outside on a bier. Simultaneously the woman closest to the deceased filled a dish with white bread and passed it across the coffin. The bread would then be given to the poor, sometimes augmented with money and cheese. With that act of Christian charity completed, everybody present knelt for the Lord's Prayer, which was repeated whenever the funeral procession reached a crossroads and when they arrived at the graveyard. As this was Wales, there could also be music, with the mourners singing psalms as they walked or at the funeral itself.

One strange custom in Wales that was also common along the Welsh Borderlands of Herefordshire and Shropshire was sin-eating. Relatives of the deceased hired a poor person to perform the duties of a sin-eater. Bread and beer were given to the poor man across the corpse, and as he ate and drank, he took on all the sins of the deceased and saved the corpse from walking after death. It was believed that every drop of wine drunk at a funeral is a sin committed by the deceased but by drinking the wine the soul of the dead is released from the burden of sin. So the moral of that belief could be: 'do what you wish as long as you can afford a decent wake.'

In some places, the mourners gave money to be distributed among the relatives of the deceased, while on the first Sunday after the funeral relatives visited the new grave. After service, the mourners placed flowers, with the herbs rue and starwort on the graves of the elderly, rocket and woodbine on less mature dead and snowdrops, primrose and violets for babies. Sadly, in the 18th and 19th centuries, there were many babies among the dead. Flowers were also placed on the graves on Flowering Sunday and on Good Friday. I had never heard of Flowering Sunday, but according to Mrs Prichard, it was another name for Palm Sunday.

It was also customary in places for the family of the deceased to send friends a small bag of arvel bread, also known as ale bread, sometimes made from barley, although sometimes more like sponge cakes. As the funeral guests ate the arvel bread, they placed a coin, usually a shilling, on the plate. A shilling (five pence) does not sound a great deal but was often a day's wage. Kipling's lines: 'Shillin' a day, It's bloomin' good pay', comes to mind. This custom was also common in the north of England, where it may be a lingering hangover from the days before the Anglo-Saxons invaded.

I will add one last death belief to finish off this section. If anybody saw blue lights in a graveyard, it was bad news, for it indicated that there would be a new grave soon. These lights were known as corpse candles and were sometimes not seen alone. It was also fairly common to see a funeral a day or so before the death.

Christmas, Boxing Day and New Year Customs

Although Charles Dickens is sometimes credited with inventing our current modes of celebrating Christmas with his famous and fabulous *A Christmas Carol*, the peak Christian winter festival was significant for many centuries before that tremendous English author. Christmas as we now know it is an amalgamation of customs and traditions from around the globe. However, the idea of celebrating Christmas is as old as Christianity while having some kind of festival in mid-winter is probably thousands of years older. Today we have Christmas decorations, the Christmas tree that Prince Albert introduced from his German homeland, and a plethora of cheap and cheerful television programmes; in old Wales things were a bit different.

Christmas celebrations started in the early morning with a church service known as Plygain or Daybreak. People would leave their house, sometimes around three in the morning, with torchlight fighting the December dark and chasing away any lingering phantoms. During the two or three-hour long service, the men would sing carols, often in complex three or four-part harmony, and then families would walk back home. Rather than exchange expensive gifts, in those more austere times, people would be much more likely to indulge in hearty eating and drinking.

Less pleasant was the Boxing Day – or St Stephen's Day – tradition of Holming, or Holly-beating. In parts of Wales, boys and young men would pick sprigs of holly and whack the bare arms and legs of girls until they bled. I wonder what the girls thought about that. In other parts of Wales, it was customary to save the sprigs of holly and the whacking for the last person out of bed. Mrs Prichard, smiling evilly, told me that when her four children were reluctant to leave their beds, she reminded them of the tradition and waved a bunch of holly around her head. 'That usually worked,' she said.

A tradition that possibly lasted from pre-Christian days was hunting the wren. According to legend, the wren was important to the Druids, and it seems that old-time sailors carried wren feathers for luck. In Wales, wrens were hunted on Boxing Day and men dressed in fancy clothes and carried the tiny prisoners from house to house. Boxing Day was also known as St Stephen Day, and one version of Stephen's story claims that a wren gave him away when he was hiding, and then he was martyred, so it was a 'Christian' thing to hunt down wrens.

One traditional Welsh ceremony is *Hel Calennig*. According to the National Museum of Wales, this was actually a New Year custom, and *Hel Calennig* means New Year's Gift. The procedure was simple and lasted from dawn until noon. The children of the community gathered into groups, carried apples decorated with evergreen sprigs and corn and walked from door to door singing songs and offering good wishes to the householders. In some areas the boys would have a bowl of water from the well and would use evergreen twigs to splash people with the water, presumably to bring luck. The use of evergreens was interesting and may again suggest a pre-Christian origin of the tradition.

In return for the songs and the free wash, the householders gave the boys sweets or money, small gifts known as *calennig*. As apples were very important to the pre-Christian Celts, this tradition may also be thousands of years old.

Hel Calennig continued at least until the 1930s in parts of West Pembrokeshire, although by then girls had joined the boys. Mrs Prichard insisted that girls had always been present, but were written out of history. The children's song has been retained:

Here we bring new water from the well so clear
For to worship God with, this happy new year'

On New Year's Day, the Welsh wanted the first person to enter the house to be dark haired and male. Redheaded people or women were seen as bad luck. It was also considered bad luck to lend money or anything else on New Year's Day.

In some villages on the last day of the year, women used to chalk patterns on their doorstep. The patterns were designed to run down the edges of the step, were often very elaborate, and sometimes passed down from generation to generation although the meanings seem to have been forgotten. The idea was for the designs to join up leaving no end or space for the devil to creep in. The belief was said to extend back to the days of the Druids.

New Year also saw gifts, with an apple very acceptable as a gift on New Year's Day, as was a loaf of bread, but what was interesting was the fact that many of these traditions had changed date. They were originally intended for the First of November, the beginning of the Celtic New Year.

Arguably the strangest custom was *Mary Lwyd*, a custom whose roots extend back far before Christianity. On the twelfth day of Christmas, or thereabouts, people thrust the skull of a horse on the end of a staff and added false eyes and ears and bells. They covered the staff with a white sheet, tied around a plethora of bright ribbons, and that was the *Mary Lwyd*. Once they had created it, people carried the *Mary Lwyd* around the community, quoting poetry at each house. The people inside also reply in verse, refusing to allow the *Mary Lwyd* entrance, and the responses, often in the form of crude insults went back and forth until the householders either allowed the horse's skull to enter or drove it away. If the party came inside, they were entertained with food and drink and then staggered off to the next house. Often the people carrying the *Mary Lwyd* became rowdy with drink, and there was petty vandalism and the occasional brawl.

As the years rolled on, the custom altered and rather than verses, the carriers of *Mary Lwyd* began to sing Christian hymns. After a long demise, the tradition shows some signs of revival. There are echoes of this poetical rivalry in the marriage customs noted above; the connection between Wales and the skills of the bard is powerful.

Lastly is a tradition that was native to the Vale of Glamorgan, west of Cardiff, where on 12th night, the people used to bake a large loaf or cake, with a ring or sometimes two, hidden inside. The oldest people in the household would split the cake into four, one section for Jesus, one for the Virgin Mary, one for the Three Wise Men and the fourth for the people present. Slices of cake were handed around and whoever had the rings became queen and king of misrule. There is a legend that claims that on this night the Druids cut mistletoe and gave it to the various tribes, with the plant retained for good fortune.

Sundry beliefs

Not all customs and beliefs can be neatly fitted into any date or category. This last section will mention a few strange beliefs that could be general across Wales, or specific to one part of the country.

The direction of the wind could be significant, with an easterly wind known as *gwynt traed y meir-w*, 'wind of the dead men's feet'. The allusion was to the direction a corpse's feet lay after burial. Apparently old women dreaded an easterly wind. Why not old men? As historically, women live longer than men, surely it would be more fateful for a man.

Fishermen and workmen in Wrexham all thought it unlucky to meet a woman while they were walking to work. Sometimes the man would simply turn around and go back home. On the other hand meeting, a dark-haired man in the morning brought good luck, as, strangely, did falling down three times while on a journey. On the other hand, it was unlucky to wear green, the Celtic mystic colour. Sometimes people who wore green thought they may have to attend a funeral soon after.

Finally, I shall add a few lines about the fate of wife beaters. In Brecon in 1881, a man who beat his wife was grabbed by a bunch of other men and tied tightly to a ladder so he could not move. He was then carried around the town and taken about three miles outside with a vast crowd gathered to watch. The men dumped the man roughly on the ground, untied him and left him there to make his own way back. Mrs Prichard added that the women of the town could throw rubbish, rotten fruit and other unpleasant objects at the beater as he was being paraded.

Wales then had a plethora of strange and not so strange customs and beliefs. Some would be centuries old, with the original function forgotten, others evolved through time and practise. All were Welsh, and the world is a less colourful place without them.

Chapter Twenty-Three
More Ghosts

Wales seemed to have ghosts peeping out from every bush and every village. For every tale I found, I had to discard twenty, and still there were plenty. This chapter has another selection, some recommended by Aelwen Prichard, others gleaned from old books, local people, newspaper accounts and some just whispered in the wind.

The Ghost of Harry Price

This story is another from Aelwen Prichard. She told me that in the early 1860s in Merthyr, there was a boy named Harry Price who saw his own ghost. According to Aelwen, Harry was a young teenager, and he left the house to go to the outside toilet and returned with his face 'as white as a sheet' and shaking. His mother asked what on earth the matter was and Harry said that he had seen his own ghost standing in the yard looking at him.

Naturally, his mother told him not to be stupid, gave him a cuff and sent him back out. There was no ghost the second time. However, within a few days, Harry took sick with fever and took to his bed. He gradually grew weaker and died.

I noted down the story, as I did all of Aelwen's stories and later I tried to find Harry Price. I did not find that name around that time, but I did find an 1864 mention in the *Aberystwyth Times* of a 14-year-old boy in Dowlais who died after apparently seeing his own ghost. The stories were too similar for coincidence, so I included it here, for although it is short, it is strangely disturbing.

The next is one of my favourites, although I have heard similar stories from other places outside Wales.

The Goblin in the Golden Cape

Some things in Wales are beyond strange. This story delves into history, mythology and national consciousness. As this book is not political, I shall avoid the latter aspect as much as possible.

As always, there is a variety of stories, all slightly different, related to the same place and event. My introduction to this story was in the *Aberystwyth Times* of August 1854, my helpful friend Aelwen Prichard added more, and the National Library of Wales helped fill in the gaps.

Apparently in 1833 workmen were repairing the roads around Mold in Flintshire. In those days there was little respect for archaeological sites, and when the workmen saw a tumulus nearby, they viewed it as a handy site for road metal rather than a hoard of priceless historical information. The workmen cheerfully removed quantities of stones until they came near to the centre of the mound when they stopped in surprise to find what the *Aberystwyth Times* called 'a skeleton of very large size'. Reports of the time said that the skull and thigh bones belonged to a man 'of great stature' but as soon as the air rushed in the bones crumbled to dust.

Losing such a skeleton was a tragedy. However, there was a consolation prize. On top of the bone-dust, where the body's chest would be, was a bright 'corset studded with 200 or 300 amber beads and crossed with a kind of filigree work.' The corset was of fine gold and contemporary opinion was it would be 'lined with fine leather.'

Speculation at the time suggested that the grave could belong to a 5th or 6th-century chieftain called Benlli Gawr, who we last met at Bardsey Island. Benlli was said to live in his fort at Moel Fenlli.

Today this fantastic artefact is known as the Mold Cape, and current opinion dates it to between 1900 and 1600 BC, making it between 3,600 and 4,000 years old. It is of solid sheet-gold from a single ingot and is held in the British Museum in London. The size of the cape would suggest it is for a woman unless the men of the period were very much smaller than they are today, so not quite the giant that the workmen initially claimed. Experts think that the Mold Cape may be connected to the nearby Great Orme copper mine.

This archaeological stuff is all very interesting, but, I hear you say there is nothing particularly strange so far, Jack. All right, how about this then: Before the discovery, the local people spoke of ghosts in glittering armour that appeared on the burial mound, so that they called the site the Field of the Goblins or the Fairy's Hill.

Now that is strange. Was there a folk memory from three thousand years before, or did the people actually see something?

According to one of the local legends, in 1830 a farmer's wife was passing by on her way back from the market in Mold. Her horse became agitated, and she saw lights glittering through the woodland on her right. As she fought to control her horse she saw a huge man in golden armour marching out of the forest, shining with a golden glow. As the farmer's wife watched, the man walked into the barrow, and the light died.

According to the story, the farmer's wife told her story to the Reverend Charles Clough, who had it included in the 1861 book *Scenes and Stories Little Known*. That book was said to be written by the Reverend's wife (it's available on Amazon or in the National Library of Wales) and is full of quirky little stories, once you get used to the writing style.

Local people called the mound *Tomen yr Ellyllon* and did not go near because of the ghosts as the field was also known as *Cae'r Yspryd*, the Field of the Ghost. There seem to be many names for that place.

Apparently, the Reverend Charles did more research and discovered that the golden ghost had been seen as far back as the 18th century, with one woman going insane after she saw it. The story of mad women is rather a recurring theme in the 19th century and so cannot be trusted entirely. It is interesting that the farmer's wife saw a huge man and the road workers said the bones they found were of a large man yet the cape is small. The giant was apparently known as *Brenin yr Allt* or the King of the Hill, and one wonders if the tales influenced the road makers' description of the skeleton they found, or if the road makers' description influenced the tales.

The vast majority of the amber beads that were found seem to have vanished, with stories that the local people or the road makers taking them away. Apparently, many of these souvenir collectors soon regretted their actions. One woman heard invisible footsteps and knocking at her window until she returned the beads to the tumulus.

What does Strange Jack believe? For what it's worth, I have heard variations of this tale right across Great Britain, usually with a golden knight haunting a burial site where later arms and armour were found. I would love to hear of an archaeological dig on a site where genuine legends are prevalent *before* any discoveries.

Ghostly Horse and Carriage

In 1887, Carnarvon was in turmoil. A phantom coach and horses had been seen rattling through the town, without even a ghostly driver. The coach first appeared as a bright light near Llanbeblig Church. As it came closer, the light metamorphosed into a single lamp shining on a dark coach hauled by a single black horse. There was nothing strange about that, except the horses' hooves made no sound, and there was no grumble of wheels on the road, and even more sinister, no driver. As the carriage passed, it left a strange glow on the road. The coach was seen vanishing through the gates of a mansion house.

When one of the observers investigated the house, he found the gates firmly locked and no sign of the coach. The mystery was never resolved.

The Return of Strongbow

When I was at the University of Dundee as a mature student, my English Professor introduced me to Wordsworth's *Tintern Abbey*. That work took a grip on me, and although the abbey did not feature in the poem, for years afterwards, I wanted to visit Tintern. In 2016 my wife and I finally got there and rather than written words, we found an architectural poem in stone. Tintern is without a doubt one of the finest, if not the finest, ruined abbey in the United Kingdom. The setting beside the River Wye and in a bowl of forested hills cannot be beaten, and the details of the stonework, combined with the overall sensation of peace, are astonishing.

Tintern was an early Cistercian foundation, dating from 1131. Unlike the Scottish Border abbeys and most places in the Welsh Marches, there is no history of raid, plunder and spoliation. Indeed Tintern enjoyed a relatively peaceful existence until Henry VIII's decision to dissolve the Catholic Church in 1536.

However, even Eden had its serpent, and Tintern has its own strange stories. One unwelcome visitor may be expected. Given such a Godly place, it is natural that the opposition should be jealous. The Devil saw all the good works that the monks of Tintern were doing and decided to prevent any more. Accordingly, he created the Devil's Pulpit nearby and preached honeyed words to entice the monks from the straight and narrow onto the broad and winding, with enough shiny gold to live any sort of lifestyle they desired. Happy at Tintern, the monks rejected the Devil's blandishments until he smiled evilly and said he could spice up the sermons for them. His idea was for a completely opposite kind of discourse, with the addition of all sorts of juicy refinements. When the monks professed interest, the Devil said he would officiate over the sermon from the abbey roof.

'Come on over,' the monks invited and the Devil, thinking that he had scored a point for the evil side, flew onto the abbey roof. As he touched down, the monks greeted him with volleys of Holy Water, which sent him back to his pulpit and maybe even to the region of brimstone and fire. That made it one – nothing for the good guys.

The Devil's Pulpit can still be visited. It is an excellent viewpoint that overlooks the abbey. Just watch out for cloven-footed gentlemen who may wish to lure you onto different paths.

For such an outstanding building, Tintern is surprisingly short of stories. The only other one I could find possibly dates from the 18th or early 19th century when the Romantic Age was at its height and 'gentlemen' – I use the term loosely- liked to poke about ancient sites to see what antiquities they could find. Two of these young hooligans arrived at Tintern with spades and high hopes as they dug in the sacred ground.

Rather than relics, they uncovered a pair of skeletons. While decent people would have re-interred the dead, the two gentlemen laughed, joked and had a celebratory meal. The two gents found it funny to speculate on what the religious monks would make of their prancing about until heavy clouds rolled in and Tintern was deluged with rain. Lightning flashed, thunder growled and the River Wye altered from smiling blue to threatening grey.

As they struggled to pack their belongings, the two men realised that a clinging grey mist had descended, shrouding the upper reaches of the abbey and slithering silently between the ancient walls and dripping trees. Through the clammy cloud, the two men saw something glowing, something that approached them, a strange light, as if a pale sun was reflecting from grey metal. They watched in horror, too scared even to back away as a figure materialised at the choir.

The light from the figure chased away the mist, so it became apparent that it was a knight in full chain mail, with a pot-helmet on his head and a longsword at his side. The knight walked, or rather glided, towards them, followed by a procession of grave-faced monks, each one wearing a hood and all evidently unhappy at these two intruders who had disturbed the graves in their holy site. According to legend, this mailed knight was none other than Strongbow, or Gilbert fitz Gilbert de Clare, earl of Pembroke. Strongbow was first to stop, with his entourage halting behind him, all in perfect silence. As the two petrified gentlemen stared, the knight drew his sword and lifted it until the point indicated the exit of the abbey. That was a sufficient hint for the two would-be antiquarians, who turned and fled, with a sudden gale throwing what remained of their meal after them.

Was this story true or even based on truth? To my mind, there are too many gothic details for it to be true. Most ghost stories are vague, with only brief sightings of the otherworldly beings, and the addition of thunder, lightning and mist are all too theatrical for reality. In saying that, knowledge of the story adds to the story of Tintern. The legend may have been started as a warning to keep treasure hunters away from Tintern, at a time when antiquities were being purloined the length and breadth of Europe and into Africa and the Middle East.

My next little offering is another warning, albeit very different.

The Abernant Ghost

Alison Lewis was dying. There was no secret about it. She knew she was dying and she was worried. She was not concerned about death or the afterlife; she had been a good Christian all her life and trusted in her faith. No, Alison Lewis was more worried about the welfare of her children after she was gone. Her husband, Evan, was not the best of fathers; in fact, he was neglectful and sometimes brutal to the children. He had already buried his first wife, and now Alison would follow her into the grave.

The family lived in Abernant near Aberdair, and it was early in 1868.

'I'll be watching from the other side,' Alison Lewis said. 'And if you don't take care of our children, I'll know all about it.'

'You'll be dead.' Unshaven and uncaring, Evan did not take his wife seriously.

Alison struggled to sit up in bed. 'If you put a single finger on my children,' she said, 'I will haunt you, and you will know all about it.'

Evan only smiled.

Inevitably, Alison Lewis died, and Evan completely forgot her threats as he concentrated on what he considered more important matters, such as drinking. He knew he had children, of course, they were the noisy creatures that infested his house, eating his food and getting under his feet, so he had to give them the odd thump now and then, push them out of the way and swear at them when occasion demanded.

He had just performed the latter operation when the jug fell from the shelf, smashing on the floor and barely missing Evan's head. He started, saw the mess and ordered his daughter to clean it up. When she was not quick enough, Evan delivered a casual slap.

'Mother is watching,' the child said, rubbing at herself.

Evan laughed at her until the chairs began to move around and the table scraped across the wooden floor.

'Who did that?' Evan demanded.

'That would be mother,' the daughter replied.

'It was you!' Evan accused.

'I'm on the other side of the room,' the daughter pointed out and ducked her father's wild swing.

When even Evan began to wonder, he called in the ex-parish constable, who understood a little about such manifestations. The constable stood in the centre of the small house and asked Mrs Lewis if she could please leave her husband in peace. He did not see from where the stone came, but he felt it as it crashed against his forehead, and he staggered back, bleeding. Quickly leaving the house, the parish constable sent for the police, who immediately suspected the innocent looking daughter.

Tying the child's hands so she could not interfere, the police dared Mrs Lewis to do anything – and the chairs began to move again.

Gradually the strange occurrences eased away, but there was never a reason found, so presumably, Mrs Lewis was at the back of things, looking after her children in death as she did in life. The lack of a reason suggests to me that the story is true, for in my admittedly limited experience; 'real' ghost stories do not have Hollywood style neat endings.

The final story in this chapter is about a town that was plagued with ghosts.

The Pencoed Ghost

At the beginning of the 20th century, the industrial town of Pencoed, between Cardiff and Swansea, seemed to be inundated with ghosts so that for a few weeks in early 1902 the town was under siege. In common with many other Welsh spirits, the Pencoed ghost, or ghosts, preferred to appear to females, so many women remained at home after dark, while those men who ventured out carried a lantern and a stout walking stick. Some men gathered into bands, armed with cudgels or other weapon as they searched for what they hoped was a hoaxer who was terrorising their womenfolk. Some of the men even planned to carry shotguns if any of the women were hurt.

Either there were many ghosts, or one who changed his appearance, for the various eyewitnesses all gave different descriptions of the spirit. Sometimes the ghost was a woman dressed all in white, sometimes a man dressed all in black and once it was a figure that was part man and part horse. Strangely, when men challenged the white woman she ran away, which was very unusual behaviour for a ghost. One man, walking from Bridgend to Pencoed found he was accompanied by a tall, dark man who walked silently alongside him in a neighbouring field.

'Who are you and what are you?' The man challenged, but the ghost did not reply.

The man returned to Pencoed, and the ghost accompanied him, always silent and the same distance away. Thoroughly alarmed, the man joined a group of horsemen and left the spirit to its own devices.

Another man met the tall, dark female. He asked her who she was and she did not reply, and then vanished. Yet another man, this time on a bicycle, met a very tall man who kept pace with him until the cyclist speeded up and the ghost disappeared. There was also a silent horseman who rode the surrounding roads.

Concerned people asked the police to help trace the ghost, partly so women could walk abroad in safety, and partly in case one of the bands of men caught it and caused serious injury. The local policeman scoured the road without success and at one point wondered if he should don woman's clothes to decoy the ghost towards him.

There was no explanation for these ghosts. They seemed to appear out of nowhere and then, suddenly, they all vanished, and the streets of Pencoed were safe again.

With that final, strange group of unsettling manifestations, it is time to close this chapter and have a brief look at Welsh Food.

Chapter Twenty-Four
Welsh Food

Sporting events are famous for the passion shown by the fans. Football and rugby supporters tend to be a bit raucous, and their chants, jibes and songs can both uplift their favourite teams and deride the opposition. Wales, of course, is famous for rugby. Indeed the Welsh rugby team is one of the best in the world. So what do the Welsh fans sing?

Guide me, O thou great Redeemer,
Pilgrim through this barren land;
I am weak, but thou art mighty;
Hold me with thy powerful hand:
Bread of heaven, bread of heaven
Feed me till I want no more.
Feed me till I want no more.

Bread of Heaven: a religious song about spiritual food and that typifies this strange country where nothing is quite what it seems. For example, in Carmarthenshire, there was laver bread or *bara lawr*, which is not bread at all. It is a species of seaweed that is eaten with shellfish or spread on toast. With a Protected Designated Origin status from the EU, this traditional Welsh delicacy has been consumed for centuries by the ordinary people of Wales. And no wonder, it is rich in protein, low in calories and tastes like oysters.

The seaweed is gathered from the coast, washed and cooked until it becomes a dark green puree or paste. Try it in spring, when there is a freshness in the air, and the hills are sharp and clear or combine it with a Welsh breakfast of bacon, eggs, laverbread and cockles, and you are fit to face the queen or work a ten-hour shift in the mines, whichever you prefer. Camden's *Britannica*, written in 1607, claimed that it has been eaten since the days of the Norse raids while the 19th-century traveller George Henry Borrow wrote of it as a hot sauce, taken with mutton. Others can eat laverbread by rolling it in oatmeal and frying it in bacon fat. It can also be used as a soup. Seaweed soup? Now that is strange.

Strange Wales even has a sculpture of Caerphilly cheese in – naturally - Caerphilly. At ten feet by three feet, the sculpture can hardly be missed. Cheese seems to have always been important in Wales, with Caerphilly cheese originating in this area, probably for the many thousands of local coal miners. Production dipped during Hitler's War and then ended utterly, with the once-Welsh cheese made in England. However, some local producers have returned, and Caerphilly is once again produced in its home country.

Possibly the best known Welsh food is Welsh Rarebit, once known as Welsh Rabbit, although, there is no rabbit in the centuries-old recipe. Here again, cheese is the main ingredient, mixed with milk and eggs. Strangely, although many restaurants within the other nations of Britain don't advertise it, Welsh rarebit is immensely popular in Japan.

Competing with rarebit for the title of Wales' national food is *Cawl*, a type of stew with Welsh lamb, leeks and potatoes. The combination of lamb, for which Wales is famous, and leeks, one of the national symbols, makes this a favourite. Finally, I will return to bread, or rather *Bara brith*, which means speckled bread. *Bara brith* is made of self-raising flour with dried fruit, mixed spices and tea.

And with the tea-flavoured bread of Welsh heaven, this little chapter will close.

Chapter Twenty-Five
Well, Well, Well

With such a chapter heading, it might be evident that there will be at least one well in this chapter. In fact, there are three.

St Winifred's Well

This well is situated at the aptly named Holywell in Flintshire. St Winifred's Well is indeed a strange place in the nicest possible way. Wales tends to hide many of her treasures, and this holy well is no exception. Although St Winnifred's Well is one of the oldest, if not *the* oldest continually visited sites for pilgrimage in the British Isles, it is not generally thought of in any casual mention of Wales.

I have seen it spelt as St Winifred's Well or as St Winefride's Well with the latter spelling coming from the Latin. Either way, the well is situated within a grade one listed building.

The legend of its origin stretches back to the year 660 AD when a particularly uncouth nobleman named Prince Caradoc fancied a beautiful young woman named Winifred. The lady did not share his feelings, so told him where to go in choicest Welsh, adding that she had decided to become a nun instead of submitting to his doubtful charms. The prince was not impressed, took his sword and chopped off Winifred's head, which, he thought, settled that particular argument. As Winifred's head bounced off the ground, a spring bubbled up and in time became known as St Winifred's Well, or more recently as the Lourdes of Wales.

What about poor headless Winifred? Well, along came her uncle, Saint Bueno. Uncle Bueno saw her predicament, stuck her head back in place and brought her back to life. Apparently, Winifred became a nun and lived for another 22 years. Now that sequence of events sounds a little unlikely, but St Beuno was a real person who spread Christianity across north Wales and according to the legend, he also called down the wrath of God on Caradoc. The Lord obliged and made the ground swallow the bad-tempered Lothario.

After having these two miracles, Bueno was tired, so had a little seat on a nearby stone and decreed that if anybody needed help, he or she should come to that very place and ask God in Winefride's name. The Lord agreed; Bueno's handy rock is still at the well and is known as Bueno's Stone.

Ever since that time, pilgrims have walked, ridden or driven to St Winifred's Well to try the waters and be cured. The site is known as one of the Seven Wonders of Wales, and a shrine was later established at the spring. Among the famous visitors was Richard 1 of England, the Lionheart, who prayed before embarking on the Third Crusade in 1189. Henry V, another English king, is said to have walked there before the Agincourt campaign in 1415, the Welshman Henry VII visited, and some of the men involved in the Gunpowder Plot prayed here before they tried mass murder: now there's a strange irony.

When James VII and II and his wife Mary of Modena had trouble creating an heir, they popped over to Winifred's place, had a little dabble and a pray, and the eventual result was young Prince James. Princess Victoria visited the well in 1828, and later became the Queen-Empress and the most important woman and probably the most important person in the world. Well, if it worked for her…

In the 15th century Lady Margaret Beaufort, benefactress of various churches, a remarkable woman and Henry VII's Mum, had a chapel built at the site. Henry VIII of England, the arch-destroyer, had the shrine wrecked in his vandalistic rampage over everything he disliked, but the well bounced back although the religious relics had gone. The exterior boasts a fantastic animal frieze. Within the shrine, the spring is strong and clear, contained inside a star-shaped pool with easy access. The surrounding vault is also worth seeing.

Is this place strange? The stories are unusual, and its survival is strange. It is even stranger that it is not better known. There are tales of at least one blind child gaining her sight. There is a story of a disabled woman regaining her ability to walk. There is a collection of crutches discarded by people who have recovered the power of their legs. There is a great deal of strange in this Lourdes of Wales.

St Tegla's Well

A few minutes' walk from the church at Llandegla in Denbighshire is St Tegla's Well, or Ffynnon Tegla, another healing well. It was the custom for people who suffered from fits to wash their hands and feet at the well during the hours of darkness. Then they would walk around the well three times intoning the Lord's Prayer. If the sufferer was a man he also had to carry a basket containing a cock, while a woman had to carry a hen; both male and female had to drop fourpence in the well. With this procedure completed, they had to walk around the church a further three times, while reciting the Lord's Prayer each circuit, and then sleep under the communal table until dawn, using the church's bible as a pillow. That was not the end of it, for they also had to put a piece of silver in the poor box and leave their fowls behind while repeating the entire procedure. After all that they surely deserved to be cured.

The Giantess and the Saint

A great many years ago, a giantess known as Caeres y Bwich lived on Bwlch y Rhiwfelen, a hill a few miles from Llandegla in Denbighshire.

In common with many giants and giantesses in the old stories, Caeres y Bwich killed and ate all the travellers on the road. Naturally, that made her very unpopular, and the local folk looked around for a white knight to help rid them of the giantess. Instead of a knight, Saint Collen came along to stop her. He armed himself and met the giant near the top of her hill.

'Who are thou' Saint Collen asked 'and why art thou here?'

The giant replied 'I myself do kill by myself.'

They fought long and hard until Collen broke the giantess's right arm. Caeres y Bwich took the right arm in her left and used it as a weapon. Collen broke her other arm, and the giantess shrieked with anger and pain. Saint Collen then killed the giantess and washed off her blood at a nearby well, known henceforth as the well of St Collen. I thought that was a strange and vaguely unsatisfying story and wondered if it was indicative of Christianity defeating paganism.

If it was or was not, that story ended the chapter of the three wells.

Chapter Twenty-Six
The Welsh Connection

For a small country, Wales has consistently punched above her weight in the world. Many people do not even realise that some great people were Welsh, or had Welsh connections. For example Tommy Cooper the comedian, Roald Dahl the author, Robert Recorde the 16th-century mathematician, Geoffrey of Monmouth who helped create King Arthur as the world recognises him, and Aneurin Bevin who invented the NHS. Welshmen and women were also instrumental in creating a country that is now part of France and in naming one of England's most celebrated icons.

Rather than run through an extremely extensive list, I shall start with a couple of people where the Welsh connection is strong. My first is an entertainer. Tommy Cooper, one of the most successful comedians of the 20th century was born in Llwyn Onn Street, Caerphilly in March 1921. His red fez and zany magic tricks became iconic to an entire generation, although he was also a serious magician as well as a tremendous entertainer. His Welsh roots should be better known.

Big Ben, the bell within the British Houses of Parliament, is also named after a Welshman. Benjamin Hall was the Baron of Llanover and Abercarn and was heavily involved in installing the bell. Hall was extremely tall, and some people believe that the bell was named in his honour.

Of course, the United States of America cannot be left out. Their Ivy League Yale University was named after Elihu Yale, who was buried at St Giles church, Wrexham. Although Yale was born in Boston, Massachusetts, Yale was from an old Welsh family from Plas yn Lal in Denbighshire. The original family name was Lal, with the nearest English equivalent being Yale. He was a significant benefactor of the then Collegiate School, and as a result in 1718 the school was renamed Yale College.

As a contrast, Sarah Morgan's name is not so often on people's lips. In fact I would doubt that one in a thousand people have ever heard of her, yet she gave birth to a son who was one of the most significant early pioneers of the United States. Sarah Jarman Morgan was from a Welsh Quaker family from Gwynedd and was born in 1700. In 1720 she married an English Quaker named Squire Boone and bore him eleven children including Daniel Boone, who opened up Kentucky and gave rise to a hundred legends and stories.

The Welsh Colonisation of Brittany

Many people believe that the 'great' in Great Britain describes a type of national pride as if the inhabitants of Britain were boasting of their power and stature. Fortunately, that belief is incorrect. The word 'great' is to contrast with the other Britain, so we have 'great' Britain, that comprises the three nations of Wales, Scotland and England, and 'lesser' Britain, which is Brittany, now part of France. How did this occur? Well, we can give most of the credit to the Welsh.

While various German tribes were careening around Europe, invading and slaughtering and generally behaving like the Goths and Vandals that some were, there was also a movement from Britain to the continent. With the pagan Saxons and Angles butchering their way across Britain, many Britons from Cornwall and Wales thought it politic to get out of the way, fast.

They took to the sea and headed east, landing in that portion of France that took their name and became Brittany. The leader of that expedition was one Conan Meriadoc, and it would be strange indeed if the wandering Welshmen did not carry their culture with them.

Centuries after their ancestors fled Wales and other parts of Britain in the face of Saxons and Angles, the peoples of Brittany were prominent in William of Normandy's invasion of England in 1066. Bretons had married Normans and were high in the social strata when they carried their lances at Hastings and the conquest of Saxon England. It is strange that the descendants of the indigenous British returned to help defeat the people who had invaded their homeland.

The next section jumps many centuries to another land and a girl who was not even Welsh. However, the Welsh connection is strong.

Alice in a Welsh Wonderland

Llandudno sits on the north coast of Wales, a premier holiday resort with a whole host of attractions that has enticed and entertained families for decades. Off the West Shore of Llandudno are two rocks. Perhaps there is nothing strange about rocks off the shore, but these two are named The Carpenter and The Walrus. You may recognise the names as both are mentioned in Lewis Carroll's famous book *Alice Through the Looking Glass*. Perhaps that simple fact would be less surprising when one realises that the real Alice was named Alice Liddell, and she spent her childhood holidays in Llandudno.

It was 1861 when eight-year-old Alice Liddell first visited Llandudno. She stayed at what is now the St Tudno Hotel on the North Shore and later at her family's holiday home of Penmorfa on the West Shore. There is a dispute whether or not Carroll ever visited Alice in Llandudno. There is no dispute that Alice told him about her adventures which were the basis for Carroll's famous books.

Llandudno, of course, capitalises on the connection with a trail through the town and a statue near the seafront of the author wearing a splendid top hat. Another man with a Welsh connection was far more powerful and possibly even stranger.

The Flagellating Tree Feller

William Ewart Gladstone was one of Britain's most prominent 19th-century prime ministers. In 1839 he came to Hawarden in North Wales and married Flint-born Catherine Glynne. Strangely, Gladstone's favourite public recreation was chopping down trees in Hawarden Park. In 1868 Queen Victoria sent him a message summoning him to Windsor in England to become Prime Minister. Before he took over the running of the nation and Empire, he finished his tree chopping.

However, Gladstone had other occupations which he was less inclined to have publicised than his vandalism of nature. As well as taking prostitutes from the streets to find them more respectable professions, the Prime Minister seems to have been a bit of a masochist. In his diaries, he admitted long conversations with the ladies of the street, after which he would whip himself. One wonders at the connection and the subject of the discussions.

So then, Wales has a fair amount of strange connections with the world. Yet there is no need to travel over water to find strangeness. Not in Wales where there is plenty of strangeness in the water.

Chapter Twenty-Seven
Stories of the Lakes

Wales is a land of hills and water. As well as the magnificent coastline, there are supposedly 398 natural lakes, which is undoubtedly sufficient for everyone in the country. Naturally, the lakes also created some strange stories.

The Lake of Many Legends

Very many years ago, I first saw the lake. I had been trekking across the Beacons with a pack on my back and mud on my boots. I was tired beyond exhaustion with every muscle screaming for relief and my stomach sure my throat had been cut days before. Rain wept from a sky of unremitting lead, and every step sloshed into watery mud, and yet I still saw the majesty and caught the magic.

Today it is known as Llangorse Lake, and it is renowned as a centre for water sports and a natural haven for wildlife. In the past, it has had many names, from Brycheiniog Mere to Llangorse Pool and Llyn Syfaddon, and it was always renowned for its legends.

Llangorse Lake is the largest natural lake in southern Wales. Situated in the Brecon Beacons, between the Black Mountains and the Central Beacons, it is a place of incredible beauty, rich in history and yet accessible for both visitors and Welsh natives alike. According to geologists, it occupies a hollow formed by ice many millennia ago. That may well be true, although the people who lived by its shores once had a much more human reason for its creation.

When Gerald of Wales was travelling through Wales in 1188, the locals told him how they believed the lake to be formed. When the world was young, the lake-dwellers claimed, the Lady of Llansafeddon was wealthy and aloof. She may also have been beautiful, the story does not say. However, a local lad fancied her, either for her looks or for her position and possibly for both. Unfortunately, the local man was poor, and the Lady of Llansafeddon barely glanced at him before scorning his offer of marriage.

Where there is a will, there is a way, and the young man ventured onto the crooked left-hand path, waylaying and murdering a merchant to grab his goods. The merchant must have been unusually wealthy for when the young man showed his new position to the Lady of Llansafeddon she was impressed.

'How did you become rich so quickly?' The Lady asked.

'I'll tell you if you promise not to tell anybody else,' the young man said.

'All right,' replied the Lady, and listened to the man's tale.

'Now will you marry me?' The man asked. Apparently, he did not think morality was high on the list of the Lady's good qualities.

'No,' the Lady said. 'First, you will have to visit the grave of the man you killed and appease his ghost.'

Still madly in lust with the Lady, the man did as she suggests. He travelled to the grave and spoke to the ghost.

As he stood there, a voice from nowhere boomed out. 'Is there no vengeance for innocent blood?'

Before the man could think of an answer, another voice sounded. 'Not until the ninth generation.' The second voice said.

The ninth generation sounded very far away so when the young man reported what had been said and the timescale of safety, the Lady agreed to the marriage. They performed the sacred ceremony and bounded eagerly into bed. Both were young, ardent and fertile so in no time their union was blessed with vibrant offspring. The couple's children were equally as productive, so grandchildren and then great-grandchildren and even great-great-grandchildren were roaming around, spreading their seeds with relish. Indeed the family grew so fast that there were soon nine generations of them all over the countryside.

'That's nine generations,' the Lady of Llansafeddon said, counting on her fingers and thankful she did not have to remove her sandals to utilise her toes. 'Nine generations and nothing ill has happened. The prophecy was wrong. Let's celebrate.'

'A feast!' Her now-not-so-young husband exclaimed, and they prepared for triumphant festivities. All the extended family was invited, and they gathered in the hollow where they had set up their home. They had houses and lands and even a church; they were wealthy and happy and uncaring of their sins. As they celebrated, the ground began to quiver and shake, the earth opened up around them, and with a great heave, it swallowed all nine generations, with all their houses and lands and all the wealth that had been so evilly gained.

As the ground sank, so water rushed in, covering the lands and buildings and sinners and hopes and dreams and all evidence of the evil. As late as the 19th century, people believed that there was a sunken town underneath the waters of the lake, and on bright days it would be possible to see the ancient buildings far underwater.

The second time I visited the lake, I knew the story, but could not see the ancient buildings. There were many other strange things around here, though. Gerald of Wales also heard about green and red currents that the lake produced to warn the local people that danger threatened, presumably attacks by the neighbouring Anglo-Norman knights. Scientists now believe these coloured currents were algal blooms, which is probably more factual, if less reassuring to people living a precarious existence on a volatile frontier.

The wonders of Llangorse Lake do not end there. In the Middle Ages, when men paddled coracles onto the lake to fish, it was believed that an afanc lived in the water, waiting to pull unsuspecting people to their deaths. In common with many such monsters, the Llangorse afanc had a name. It was known as Gorsey, although I suspect that the name came long after the fear and possibly the belief had subsided. Lewys Glyn Cothi, also known as Llywelyn y Glyn, a fifteenth-century poet, mentioned the afanc.

> '*The afanc am I, who, sought for, bides*
> *In hiding on the edge of the lake.*'

I don't think this particular monster has been seen in recent years. Like the Scottish Nessie, it is more a creature to be spoken about than to be seen.

After that brief mention of coracle fishing, this seems a good place to mention that strange craft. There is a of coracle fishing in various Welsh waters, including the River Towy. Coracles are river vessels indigenous to Britain although now mainly, possibly exclusively used in Wales. The Irish curragh is similar but larger. The Welsh coracles are constructed with a framework of ash or hazel, about a metre wide by one and a half metres in length. Today pitched canvas is stretched over the frame although originally it would have been animal hides, bull or cow.

Coracles are light, so one man can carry them on his back and are used for fishing in the Towy and other Welsh rivers. The system is centuries old, with two coracles working together with a net between them. I am fully aware that coracle fishing may not be regarded as strange, but the retention of this ancient practice is too impressive to ignore.

To return to Llangorse Lake: even less known is the secret door in the rocks nearby. According to legend, somewhere in the surroundings of the lake, there is a door to another world, or perhaps another dimension. This door only appeared on one day each year, and if one was fortunate, one could see into fairyland. The door opened into a small island in the middle of the lake where the fairies lived.

Strangely enough, there is an island in the lake, but rather than fairies it is thought that a local king resided here when things outside were dangerous. The correct term for this artificial island is a crannog, and it is a thousand years old. Perhaps such an island encouraged stories about the fairies.

Lastly in this strange place is the story of the old lady, a tale that harks back to the Lady of Llansafeddon. According to the legend, there are times when the steeple of a church protrudes above the water, and an old woman perches on the weathercock. She is the known as the Old woman of Llangors, and she used to entice children to her.

'Come along, my little child' she would say, and the child would walk willingly into her grasp only for child, woman, weathercock, steeple and Uncle Tom Cobley and all to vanish beneath the waters of the lake. Was this story created to warn children not to go near the edge of the lake, a folk memory of the lake monster, or a garbled version of the sunken village story? We will never know for sure, but it does bring a shiver of mystery to this lovely Welsh lake.

Don't Trust the Lady

Also in the Brecon Beacons, at Llyn Cwm Llwch, near a secret door into another island of fairyland, there is an elderly woman. This lady sings the most wonderful songs and plays the most beautiful tunes on her harp. Indeed she is so enchanting that people follow her music as if she was the pied piper. They walk into the waters of the lake and drown. This woman is more than your average mass murderer though, for she kills with a purpose. As soon as she has drowned nine hundred people, she will be young again so be very careful if you venture close.

There is another legend associated with this lake. At one time in the past, men attempted to drain the lake to find the fairies' treasure. As they did so an old man emerged from the waters and issued a stark warning:

If you disturb my peace,
Be warned that I will drown
The valley of the Usk,
Beginning with Brecon town

The attempt to drain the lake ended and humankind has not tried again. Best leave well alone!

Another Lake with a Beautiful Woman

Not far from Llandovery in Carmarthenshire is a picturesque lake known as Llyn-y-Fach, which holds a strange little legend. One day, many centuries ago, a cowherd was tending his cattle by the lake when there was a commotion in the water and the most beautiful woman he had ever seen emerged. She smiled at the astonished herd and slid back beneath the gentle waves. The herd had been too surprised to speak but returned to the spot time after time hoping to see something of the lady again.

He had almost given up hope when she rose again, smiling so alluringly that his heart nearly failed him and he was left tongue-tied. However he did not give up, and on a third occasion she appeared, and he spoke to her. He knew that he was in love and asked for her hand in marriage.

The lady of the lake agreed, with two conditions: one was that he should never tell anybody where she came from, something to which he agreed at once. The second was that if ever he struck her three times she would return to the lake, taking with her all their worldly goods. The herd agreed as he had no intention of ever hitting such a beautiful woman. It was evident that the lady was not a mortal, but the herd did not care if she was a fairy, a goddess, or a witch, as long as she became his wife.

This story holds a faint echo of an ancient Welsh law that banned a man from hitting his wife unless she had committed a grave crime, and then he could only hit her a maximum of three times.

The couple married and lived happily together, with their fortune increasing and the herd's reputation and standing growing year after year. The couple raised three handsome sons together – and there the legend splits. One version says that prosperity and success made the herd big-headed and he began to neglect his old friends and renege on his promises. As his reputation dipped, he became foul tempered, and after a failed business deal he slapped his wife.

She stepped back, holding her face, and reminded him of their marriage contract. Shocked at his behaviour, he asked her forgiveness, which she immediately granted, but things were not as they had been. On two more occasions he slapped her, and on the third, she reminded him of their agreement and left the marriage, with all the animals following her into the water.

Another version says that he did not slap her and did not become bad-tempered. Instead, the herd gave his wife a friendly pat with his gloves and then patted her shoulder in sympathy as she cried over a baby whose life she knew would be short. He tried his best not to tap her again but failed when they attended the child's funeral. The wife was smiling, and the herd tapped her shoulder to ask why she was happy at a funeral. The wife said she was pleased because she knew the child was happy in the next place, but that was the third strike, and she left with all the livestock.

However, there is a happier postscript. The three sons became great and famous healers, no doubt with powers inherited from their mother.

As I have mentioned fairies a few times, this is as good a place as any to add a little explanation. In Wales, fairies were often termed *Tylwyth Teg*, meaning the good folk although they were anything but good, being mischievous little devils. They were rife in the countryside, plaguing people in their cottages, turning milk sour and spilling their drinks, keeping old women awake in bed and mocking whatever they did. There are stories that even in the middle of the 19th-century people believed in such things and erected barriers of gorse even inside their cottages to keep the naughty fairies from molesting them.

Of course, Welsh fairies were different from those in other nations. While English fairies travelled by broomstick and Scottish fairies on eggshells, the more sensible Welsh fairies hitched a lift on the back of a corgi dog.

Lost City

Bala Lake, or Llyn Tegid to use its proper name, is the largest natural lake in all of Wales and is another lake that hides more than one secret. One is the monster that is said to lurk under the waters, waiting for an unwary human to come within its reach. The local folk call it Teggie and claim that it looks a bit like a crocodile. However Teggie the Bala crocodile is not alone for he shares the unseen bottom of the lake with the court and town of Tegid Foel. Apparently, Tegid was married to Ceridwen, who was either a witch or a goddess or perhaps both. The happy couple lived in a palace surrounded by a town, and then one night an unexpected flood inundated town and palace and people and all.

Naturally, if you choose to visit on the night of a full moon, you may be fortunate enough to see the lights of Tegid and Ceridwen's court. Is this legend another folk memory of an actual event of centuries ago? It seems strange that there should be so many similar legends in such a small geographical area.

Now here we touch genuine strange for Llyn Tegid is the only place in the world where the gwyniad fish lives. According to the scientists, this species was trapped in Tegid during the last Ice Age and is still there now, 10,000 years later. This fish is too small to be accused of being Teggie, but gives rise to the question: what if some other ancient creature was trapped in the lake 10,000 years ago and folk memory retained the image? Just a thought.

So that was a rapid tour of only a few of Wales' nearly 400 lakes. I will finish with a tale of the mountains, partly to prove I am not biased, and mainly because it is too good a tale to leave out.

The Giant of Cadair Idris

Although it is now popular with walkers, Cadair Idris was once a place best avoided for many reasons. Cadair Idris is a mountain in Snowdonia, with the name meaning the Chair of Idris, who was a giant, a warrior and – this being Wales – also a poet. Some people link Idris with Arthur, while others used to claim that there were so many fairies around this hill that it was best to avoid it after dark. If one falls asleep here, one could wake up insane, or perhaps become a poetical genius, which is not far off insanity. Possibly even more sinister was the legend that Gwyn ap Nudd, who ruled the Otherworld and his pack of Cwn Annwm lived here, scouring the area for souls. The Cwm Annwm were spectral hounds and definitely best avoided Even recently people have seen lights hovering around the summit in mid-winter. Nearby Llyn Cau is said to be bottomless and the home of a monster that drowns swimmers. I had to put in a lake to close this chapter of lakes.

Chapter Twenty-Eight
Musical Wales

Wales is justly famous for its music, which appears in various places and guises throughout this book from singing at weddings and rugby matches to psalms at funerals.

Sometimes the music is ghostly. Wales seems to have more supernatural music than other parts of Britain. For instance, at Llandysul on the River Teifi, there is a small section named the Pool of the Harper where a musician is said to have drowned. The sound of her or his harp can still be heard by some, but details are scanty. Pendine on Carmarthen Bay is another of these Welsh villages that hides so much, from attempts on the land speed record to earth tremors. There are many caves in the limestone, and some people have found bones and teeth here. Not far away is Gilman's Point, where a mermaid was once seen, and one of the cliffs contains Green Bridge Cave where a fiddler entered, playing his fiddle. He never returned, and sometimes his music is still heard, a warning to be careful inside the cave system.

There is another musical cave at Criccieth in Gwynedd where a pair of wandering musicians saw two beautiful women. The musicians followed the women into a cave, only to find the women were fairies who had trapped them there forever. The pair still play their music as a warning to others. Other ghostly music is friendlier, such as the music that eases from beneath the ruins of the 12th century Talley

Abbey in Carmarthenshire. Then there is the phantom organist of Old Stradey House, who may, or may not, be Lady Mansel who is one of the many ghosts said to haunt the place. Raglan Castle in Gwent is also haunted, with the music of a ghostly bard. He is supposed to be more often seen or heard where the old library used to be and could be William Herbert the first earl of Pembroke. Either the atmosphere in Wales has affected the spectres, or they were Welsh, to begin with, with music in their spirit.

Valle Crucis Abbey in Llangollen also has the music of unseen chanting monks. There are other strange manifestations in the abbey, such as the stonework at the front of the abbey being lit up, or warriors in golden armour appearing, one of whom might be Owain Glyndwr, one of Wales' foremost freedom fighters.

Fairies, naturally, are renowned for their music right across Wales. For instance in Pentraeth in Anglesey, the fairies on the small hill of Mynydd Llwydiarth sing without being seen, and the Twm Barlwm Hill Fort near Pontypool is also the scene of fairy music. When children try to investigate, the fairies take them into the hill, never to be seen again. After so many thousand years of contact between fairies and humans, one would think that people would learn to keep their children safe. It is very simple, folks: look after your children and don't let them wander off with strange fairies.

One instrument the Welsh are famed for is the harp. Of course, being Welsh, they have to be different. While most harps have a single row of strings, the Welsh harp has three. Strangely, the Welsh harp is not actually Welsh. It was invented in Italy in the 17th century and not until the 18th was it thought of as Welsh. Before that date, Welsh harpers used a much more common instrument.

This may seem to be the wrong place to put in a word about what is possibly the most familiar nickname for a Welshman, but bear with me. It was the English who first called the Welsh Taffy or Taff. It is possible that the name originated from an inability to correctly pronounce the Welsh name Dafydd, or it could be that the outsiders referred to people who lived near the banks of the River Taff that flows through Cardiff. The first recorded use seems to be in the middle of the 18th century although it may have been in common usage long before. There is another theory that the name could derive from Amacthon, a Celtic god, although that is a bit farfetched, even for this book.

There is an oft-repeated piece of doggerel that begins:

Taffy was a Welshman, Taffy was a thief

The poem continues with a variety of anti-Welsh insults which have no place in this book or anywhere else. In the 19th century, the London-based magazine *Punch* gave a response with its *Ode to Wales*.

I went to Taffy's house, many things I saw
Cleanliness and Godliness, obedience to the law
If Taffy rode to my house, or unto Pat's should swim
I think my Taffy would observe that we might learn of him.'

These few lines do not redress the balance, but perhaps they show a glimmering of awareness of the quality that Wales possesses. My final chapter here will hopefully show something of the variety of Welsh strangeness, with a selection of anecdotes that did not fit into any specific category.

Chapter Twenty-Nine
And Finally

This chapter is even more of a hodgepodge of the diverse and the odd. Most of the pieces are very short and lacking in detail yet I think they have sufficient interest to be included. I will begin with a couple of sports that are not exactly mainstream.

Strange Sports

Every nation has a quota of strange sports and Wales is no exception. In a country obsessed with rugby and whose football team can often produce an upset against sides with far greater demographic and financial assets, Welshmen and women can occasionally turn to other recreational occupations, one of which is Shin Kicking. Also known as 'purring', this sport must be one of the strangest and most painful ever invented. It is quite simple. All you need is an opponent, a pair of boots and an incredible tolerance for pain. The rules are equally simple. Lock arms with one's opponent, face him or her and then the pair of you kick lumps out of each other's shins until somebody falls down.

It appears that this sport originated among Welsh miners in the 17th century (although the English also claim it) and lasted until the early 20th century, to be revived in a gentler form in 1951. It spread from Wales to Cornwall and then England, with one notable match in

England in 1843 when two men, stark naked except for heavy boots, hacked at each other for full three-quarters of an hour.

According to folklore, some competitors died from the results and more were crippled for life. It was said that some Welsh shin-kickers had nails pointing from the sides of their boots. Today it is a much more civilised sport, with soft shoes worn and the participants allowed to have padding on their shins.

As a welcome relief, why not try Bog Snorkelling. Even the name would put me off, but some people enjoy this strange sport. Every year, the World Bog Snorkelling Championships take place at Llanwrtyd Wells in Powys. Bog snorkelling must surely be one of the most bizarre sports anywhere. The idea is to race along two 55-metre long trenches hacked through a peat bog. The rules state that the swimmers wear snorkels and only use flippers to propel themselves.

Despite Wales' ancient attraction to sports, bog-snorkelling is new, with the first World Championship held in 1985 at the Waen Rhydd peat bog at Llanwrtyd Wells. There is also Mountain Bike Bog Snorkelling and even a Bog Snorkelling Triathlon, with snorkelling, bike riding and running. You can't get much stranger than this sport, surely.

My next little piece is about Cardiff in the 1850s.

Strange Coincidence

As with all cities, Cardiff has expanded in the last hundred and fifty years, taking over much land that was once rural. In the process, much local folklore has been forgotten, and the old stories have been lost. Hopefully this small piece will remain with us.

Around the early summer of 1857, a house named the Sweldon in the parish of Caerau was severely damaged by fire. At that time it was about four miles outside Cardiff, not far off the Cowbridge Road. Both names still exist although the locality has altered tremendously. Even before it burned, local people gave the Sweldon a wide berth. Rumours abounded, stories that it had been a church before it was converted to a house, and much worse, tales that ghosts and other creatures roamed about the garden, with spectral encounters in the orchard. Even so, the house was tenanted, with a farmer and his wife paying to stay in this strange building. After the fire, the house was renovated, with the plaster stripped from the bare stonework. During the renovations, a hidden chamber was discovered with the remains of two bodies, right next to the bedroom which the farmer and his wife had occupied. Strangely, once the bodies were found, the sightings of ghosts and other things immediately ended.

A Welsh Springheel Jack

Springheel Jack was one of the bogeymen of the 19th century. Nobody knows what or who he was if it was one man or many men, if he was natural or supernatural, troublemakers playing tricks or the devil himself. He appeared at various times to slap, punch, poke or prod at people, mostly but not exclusively women, then bounded away over walls and up the sides of building as if he had springs in his shoes, hence the name, Springheel Jack.

In 1887 Jack appeared in Chirk in Denbighshire. Or rather a pretend Jack tried to fool people by bounding from a graveyard dressed in a sheet. The locals in Chirk were not so easily fooled and greeted him with a volley of stones that sent him bouncing away.

A more believable Jack arrived on the North Caernarvonshire coast the following year. This Jack appeared to lone women with exhibitions of bounding and loud cries, he terrorised men walking to their work in the wee small hours and generally made a pest of himself. One bazaar proprietor decided to profit from the general panic and claimed to have caught Jack and showed an acrobatic young man to those gullible customers who paid the entrance fee. Few people were fooled. The police searched for Jack, who vanished as suddenly as he had appeared.

Ten years later Jack was in Neath. At first, he continued with his foolery, tapping at windows, making strange cries to women and leaping over walls. In November he broke into the house of a hairdresser named Newton and attacked a young servant girl. The jesting stopped when this Jack crept behind the girl, ripped her clothing off from shoulders to hem and cut her face, as well as smearing her cheeks with blacking. Not surprisingly the girl became hysterical. Jack also attacked a lady's companion at the gates of Eaglesbush House, saying that if she did not stop screaming, he would gag her 'but if you're quiet, I'll let you go.'

The woman obeyed, and Jack bounded away, to return a moment later, raise his hat politely and vanish. People hoped he had gone for good but in the early months of 1900, Springheel Jack made an appearance in Aberystwyth.

Jack waited on a lonely road just outside the town, appearing to travellers out of nowhere, leaping over 12 foot high walls, terrifying women and on at least one occasion, attacking a lone man. The authorities could have laughed this creature off as superstitious nonsense but instead ordered the army to patrol the road and deal with whatever they found.

Happy to have something useful to do, the soldiers patrolled with great enthusiasm, questioning every passer-by they met, prodding bayonets into hedges and generally making themselves more of a nuisance than bouncing Jack ever was. However, with the army's presence, the sightings of Jack ended, and peace returned to Aberystwyth. People's nerves settled, and Springheel Jack became a bit of a joke. And that seems to have been the last that Wales saw of Springheel Jack, or of the men who copied him.

Was Jack supernatural? Or did a succession of strange men latch onto the name to terrorise people? That question remains unanswered.

Welsh Eccentrics

It is usually the English who are thought to have most eccentrics. However, Wales has its own quota of historical eccentricities, proving that strangeness is not monopolised by any one country. I will only mention a couple, such as Viscount Tredegar, who was only one member of a strange family. According to legend, the mother of the Second Viscount thought she was a kingfisher and proved it by building herself a bird's nest and sitting within it. However, she was also generous to charities so we can forgive her little foibles, if they are correct and not manufactured. Her son, Evan Frederick Morgan, who became Viscount Tredegar, was also a bit of a bird fancier, with a pet macaw to join his baboon and kangaroo at his Newport home. Nothing extraordinary about that, perhaps, but his party trick was to train Blue Boy, his pet parrot, to crawl inside his trousers and thrust his head through his open flies. Apparently, some women did not appreciate this strange appearance.

Although he married twice, Evan was also a homosexual who actively hunted young men in North Africa and Bali. He stood as the Conservative MP at Limehouse in 1929 and had a room in Tredegar House where he studied the occult. Indeed, the Viscount Tredegar was a strange man.

So too was the 5th Marques of Anglesey, often known as Toppy. In 1898, aged a young 23 years, he fell heir to both the title and the family fortune. Before the first decade of the 20th century was spent, so was all his money.

The family made their fortune through coal mines, and Toppy spent it on jewels and boats, furs and horses. He also married but was too preoccupied with his own narcissism to spend time in bed with his wife. After three years she divorced him with their marriage still unconsummated. Driving in a car whose exhaust emitted perfume, he bought his own theatre company so people could see him perform. This so-called Dancing Marques created the 'butterfly dance' to show off his hip movements.

Is it wealth that creates such eccentricity? Or do we all have a streak of strangeness, but only wealth allows us to indulge in our strange conceits? I think that possessing wealth gives people the freedom to step clear of public opinion and act as they wish without conventional restrictions. However, our next strange tale has us return to Cardiff and a case of grave robbing.

Robbing a grave

Cardiff is not renowned for sensationalism. It is a sensible, hardwork-
ing city yet in July 1868 there was a case that involved both second
sight and grave robbing. The principal character was a professional
clown named James Fagan who was married to a younger, attractive
woman. His wife caught consumption, was admitted to the infirmary
and died. Naturally upset, Fagan saw her decently buried at the Old
Cemetery at the beginning of July and returned home to mourn his
loss.

However, his nights were troubled by dreams that somebody was
digging up his wife's coffin, and during the day he had a disturbing
feeling as if his wife was pulling at him, begging for help. Asking
his brother-in-law to accompany him, Fagan walked to the cemetery
in the evening, just as the shadows were lengthening and darkness
cloaking the gravestones.

The gate was locked, so the pair peered through the iron railings,
trying to see Mrs Fagan's grave, which was too far from the entrance
to be easily visible. When one of the attendants asked if the two men
wished to enter, they agreed and walked through the rows of graves.

Exactly as Fagan had dreamed, the grave gaped open, and he hurried
over, just in time to catch a man in a white coat working on the top
of the coffin, unscrewing something from the lid. Fagan challenged
him and hauled him to the surface, at which point the man began to
shovel earth back into the grave. When Fagan asked him if he was
the gravedigger, the man replied 'no' and ran away. More concerned
about his wife than the culprit, Fagan entered the grave and found
that the breastplate of the coffin had been removed, as well as one of
the end plates.

The police arrested the gravedigger, James Barratt, who was the
man in question. He said a stranger had paid him two shillings to dig
up the grave. Fagan mentioned that his wife liked to wear jewellery
and Barratt might have thought she was still wearing it when she was
buried. I wish there were more details for this case, with the grave

robbing and more interestingly, the possible second sight or a voice from beyond the grave. Anywhere else, such an incident might have created much comment. In Wales it was accepted as normal.

And that is the end of Jack Strange's book of strange Wales. I hope that you found it even half as enjoyable to read as I found it to research and write. For every ghost included, at least ten were left out, and I barely touched the castles, mountains and lakes. Wales is a country of constant surprises, with so much hidden from the casual visitor. It is a country where everything has a song; the surf chants as it breaks on the shore, the rivers sing in their secret solitude through the hills, and even the wind whispers to its own tune.

To understand Wales, go to the Principality Stadium when the Welsh rugby team are playing a major game. I defy you not to have shivers running up your spine when the crowd sings *Bread of Heaven*. Or visit the Cambrian Mountains in the darkening of a blustery October evening when the clouds are slithering across the hills and the bleat of sheep echo from the slopes. Or go to the Wild West coast and look out to sea as the sun sets behind the islands. Or visit the Valleys in the pinking flush of a winter dawn, where rows of ex- miners' cottages are ranked like soldiers on parade, hiding the strength and tragedies of the men who tore black gold from the ground at such terrible cost.

That is Wales; that is Cymru, one of the strangest countries in the world. I love it.

Jack Strange
Aberystwyth, August 2018

Books by the Author

It's A Strange Place, England
Strange Tales of Scotland
Strange Tales of the Sea
The Strangeness That is Wales

47202558R00122

Printed in Poland
by Amazon Fulfillment
Poland Sp. z o.o., Wrocław